# Impressions & Experiences of a French Cavalry Trooper

# Impressions & Experiences of a French Cavalry Trooper

## During the First World War, 1914-15, With the 22nd Dragoons

## ILLUSTRATED

## Christian Mallet

**LEONAUR**

*Impressions & Experiences of a French Cavalry Trooper*
*During the First World War, 1914-15, With the 22nd Dragoons*
by Christian Mallet

ILLUSTRATED

First published under the title
*Impressions and Experiences of a French Trooper, 1914-15*

Leonaur is an imprint of Oakpast Ltd

Copyright in this form © 2020 Oakpast Ltd

ISBN: 978-1-78282-914-0 (hardcover)
ISBN: 978-1-78282-915-7 (softcover)

http://www.leonaur.com

Publisher's Notes

# Contents

NIGHT CHARGE OF THE 22ND DRAGOONS, SEPT. 10-11, 1914.

In Memoriam
To My Captain
Count J. De Tarragon
And
To My Two Comrades
2nd Lieut. Magrin and 2nd Lieut. Clère
With Whom
Many Pages of This Book are Concerned
Who Fell
All Three on the Field of Honour
In Defence
Of Their Country

*"Dragons que Rome eut pris pour des Légionnaires."*

# Frontispiece

This picture by Carrey represents the night charge of a squadron of 22nd Dragoons against German trenches near Compiègne. During the night of September 9th, the squadron leader, who had received orders to endeavour to intercept and capture a large enemy convoy, suddenly came under a hot fire from German trenches. In the darkness it was impossible to choose his country, but the position before him must be attacked, and, signalling the charge, he led his squadron at the trenches. As the first line rose to the jump the Germans scuttled out in panic, only to be ridden down and destroyed.

With the 22nd are shown two troopers of the 4th Dragoon Guards, belonging to the 2nd British Cavalry Brigade. Both had fought at Mons, but during the retirement had lost their regiment, and after wandering about for some days fallen in with the 22nd Dragoons and fought for some weeks in their ranks. Whilst still under heavy fire, one of these Englishmen, throwing the reins of his horse to his companion, dismounted and ran to and rescued a French trooper whose horse had fallen dead and pinned him to the ground; on rejoining their own regiment their French commanding officer gave them the following certificate of service:

I, the undersigned, certify that T..... and B ...., troopers, belonging to the 4th Dragoon Guards, lost themselves in the neighbourhood of Péronne on the 20th August, and joined up with my squadron, and have since then formed part of it and engaged in all its operations. On the night September 10-11 my squadron received orders to capture a German convoy, and found itself surrounded by the re-treating enemy.

T..... and B .... took part in a charge by night against entrenched infantry, and helped in the fighting on the outskirts of the forest of Compiègne.

They are both men of fine courage and high training, and have given me every satisfaction.

(Signed)                                                A. De S.,
Captain, 22nd Dragoons.

(*Le Temps*,)

# The 22nd Regiment of Dragoons

| | |
|---|---|
| Austerlitz | 1805 |
| Jena | 1806 |
| Eylau | 1807 |
| Oporto | 1809 |

The 22nd Regiment of Dragoons was raised in 1635 under the name of "The Orleans Regiment," and took part from 1639 to 1756 in all the great wars in which the French were engaged before the Revolution. From 1793 to 1814 the regiment was continually at work, first under the Republic and then in Napoleon's armies.

It saw service in the Army of the Sambre and Meuse, 1794-1796; the Army of the Rhine, 1800; the *GrandeArmée*, 1805; in the war in Spain, 1808-1813; the Campaign in Saxony, 1813; the Campaign in France, 1814.

The regiment was disbanded in May, 1815, and was not raised again until September, 1873.

# Chapter 1

# Mobilisation

Of all my experiences, of all the unforgettable memories which the war has woven with threads of fire unquenchable in my mind, of all the hours of feverish expectancy, joy, pain, anguish and glorious action, none stands out—nor ever will—more clearly in my recollection than the day when we marched out of Rheims. Nothing remains, except a confusion of disconnected memories of the days of waiting and of expectation, days nevertheless when one's heart beat fast and loud. A bugle-call sounding the "fall-in" lifts the curtain on a new act in which, the empty years behind us, we are spurring our horses on into the eternal battle between life and death.

On the thirtieth of July, 1914, I did not believe in the possibility either of war or of mobilisation—nor even of partial mobilisation—and I refused to let my thoughts dwell on it.

The good folk of Rheims, excited and anxious, gathered from time to time in dense crowds outside the building of the *Societé Genérale*, on the walls of which the latest telegrams were posted up, then broke up into knots of people who discussed the situation with anxiety and even consternation. At the Lion d'Or, where I turned in for dinner on the terrace under the very shadow of the cathedral, I called for a bottle of Pommery, saying jocularly that I must just once more drink champagne; a message telephoned from a big Paris newspaper reassured me, and in the peaceful quiet of a fine summer's night I returned to my quarters with a light heart.

As I was turning into bed, I caught a glimpse through the barrack window of the two Gothic towers of the cathedral, standing high above the city as if in the act of blessing and guarding it.

All was quiet: the silence was only broken from time to time by the cry of the swallows as they skimmed through the clear air.

War, I repeated to myself, it is foolish even to think of, and this talk of war is but the outcome of some disordered pessimistic minds; and with that I went to sleep on my hard, little webbed bed . . . for the last time.

Towards midnight I woke with a start, as though someone had shaken me roughly. Yet all was still: the barracks were rapt in sleep. Nearby me only the loud and heavy breathing of the twelve men who made up the number occupying the room could be heard, as I lay on my back, wide awake, waiting, for I now felt that the signal would surely come which should turn the barracks into a very hive of bees.

Five minutes passed—perhaps ten—then a deafening bugle call which made the very walls vibrate, calling first the first squadron, growing in volume as it called the second, louder still the third, like the roar of some beast of prey as it summoned ours; then it died away as it got farther off across the barrack square where the fifth squadron was quartered.

It was the call to arms.

The sleepy troopers, half awake, sat up in their beds with a start—"Hulloa!—what? What is the matter? . . . Are we really mobilising?"

Then followed the sound of heavy boots in the corridors, heavy knocks on the doors, the silence of the night was a thing of the past and had given place to deafening clatter.

In a few seconds every man was on his feet without any clear idea as to what was forward. The sergeant-major called to me: "Mallet—run and warn the officers of the squadron to strap on their mess tins with their equipment and assemble in barracks as quickly as possible."

So, it's serious, is it? and in a flash the truth, the very reverse of what I had been trying to believe, forced itself upon me and paralysed all other power of thought. Whether it breaks out to-morrow or in a month's time, it is war—relentless war—that I seem to see like a living picture revealed.

The impression masters my mind as I turn each corner of the dark streets and open spaces, and the cathedral with its twin towers, so peacefully standing there, is transformed into a giant fortress watching over the safety of the countryside.

A man comes out of a house on the place and runs after me, I hear his heavy shoes striking the pavement behind me; breathless he blurts out the question, "Is war declared?"

"War . . . yes . . . that is to say, I don't know."

I continue on my way to carry out my orders with enough time left to run up to my own rooms and get some money and clean linen.

I got back to barracks as dawn was spreading over the sky, and found our commandeered horses being brought in by civilians and soldiers in fatigue overalls. An elderly non-commissioned officer shrugged his shoulders and said in a low voice, "Commandeered horses being brought in already!—that does not look very healthy."

At the time of the Agadir affair things did not get as far as that, and the incident forced itself on my mind as proof that war was inevitable.

Packing and preparation were over and the men, waiting for orders, were wandering about the square, and in the canteen, which they filled—still half dark as it was—one heard shouts of joy and high-pitched voices telling the oldest and most threadbare stories.

But the canteen-keeper—friend of us all—with red eyes and shaking voice, was talking of Bazeille, her own village, burned by the Germans in 1870, where her old father and mother still lived. She is horrified at the thought of another invasion of the soil of France.

"The Bosches here? No, indeed, Flora, you are talking wildly; never you doubt, we will send them to the right-about and back to Berlin at the point of our toes—give us another glass of white wine—the best—that's better worth doing."

"Well, well!"

At the table where I sat with my own particular friends, all were in high spirits, all talking the greatest nonsense, becoming intoxicated with their own words as they romanced of heroic charges, of wonderful forced marches and highly fantastic battles; I alone remained somewhat serious and heavy of heart, and abused myself for being less free of care than they in the face of this triumph of manliness and youthful high spirits; yet in spite of myself, I watched them, these comrades of mine, day in, day out, to whom I should become more closely allied still by war, and tried to pierce the mists of the future, grey and threatening, and to discern what was to be the fate of each.

There they sat: Polignac, who was to be taken prisoner a short four weeks later, and who still languishes in a Westphalian fortress; Laperrade, who was to fall dead with a lance head through his chest as he defended his officer; Magrin, fated to die, when spring came, with a bullet through his heart; Clère, whom death was to claim three days after having heroically won his commission, and all the rest of them, too many to name here, but of all of whom I cherish in my heart a recollection not only tender but full of pride that they were my friends.

Yet the day passed in a fever of expectation and excitement. The smallest piece of news, or the greatest absurdity told by the latest man from the guard-room of the 5th, or the stables of the 2nd, or by "the adjutant's orderly," flew like the wind round the barracks, increased in volume, became distorted, took shape no one knew how and in the end was believed by all—until some still more ridiculous tale took its place.

There were waggish fellows, too, who wandered from group to group with a serious look on their faces, saying, "Well, it's come now; I have just heard the colonel give the order to stand to horses," and until evening, when we were again crowded inside the canteen, it was the same hunger for news, the same excitement, the same desperate longing to know what was happening.

Only at seven o'clock did we get the official news, and although it came as no surprise, the whole barrack was stunned by it. Squadron orders issued at seven o'clock gave us three hours to prepare to march, as prescribed by the rules governing the movements of covering troops, to which we belonged. In three hours we should be on the way to an unknown destination; to ourselves fell the honour of being the advance guard; to us the task of guarding and watching the frontiers whilst the rest of the army was mobilising; and with keen pride in the fact, we held up our heads and thrust out our chests, whilst our faces took on a look of confidence in our power to conquer. Even the humblest trooper seemed transfigured, and in that moment I realised, perhaps for the first time, the high soul of France.

But the news soon spread beyond the barracks. Rheims, although some twenty minutes' walk away, somehow learned it, and almost immediately all the town flocked to the barrack gates. I say all the town because all classes together hurried there pell-mell—not only those with a brother or son or a friend amongst the troops about to set off, but those who were drawn by ties of friendship with the regiment, and those who came from mere curiosity. The crowd, which got larger and larger, beat upon the iron gates like waves breaking vast and black on a rocky shore.

Old women came to give a last kiss to their sons; old men, too, pensioners who had fought in '70, whose hands trembled as they pressed those of their boys, distracted little shop girls who held their lovers passionately in their arms—silk frocks and broadcloth mingled together in one vast crowd swayed by deep emotion, brave and placid, though its heart was near breaking—every sob was stifled, every mouth drawn with sorrow yet tried to laugh, and it was cheerily that the last partings took place, the last touching and heartfelt "God speed" was said.

How great a country to possess such children! Soon the gates could no longer bar the passage of the crowd which swept like a torrent through the outer square, overwhelmed the sentries, and threatened to engulf everything.

As the hour of departure grew nearer, the farewells became more animated. Then the bugles sounded through the barracks the order for "majors to join the colonel," next captains and others of commissioned rank; there was a scurrying of officers to and fro before the orderly room, and Colonel Robillot himself could be seen standing on the doorstep watching the scene with a look of pride and indulgence in his eyes.

At nine o'clock, as I was standing some distance apart in a corner of the square with friends who had come to bid me a last farewell, a non-commissioned officer, touching me on the shoulder, warned me that my troop was about to fall in, and I had to break off my *adieux*.

From that moment I was to think no more of myself. All was over with affairs that bound heart or fancy. The supreme moment had come when words no longer count, and when the eyes try to fill themselves with one last gaze upon those whom one is leaving—goodbye to family, to love, to self, to the joy of the living—all one's soul goes out in this last gaze.

This look would say, "Farewell, I will be brave, never doubt it, don't cry, don't suffer regrets." This look embraces all that life has meant up to now, whether of joy or sorrow. It is final—a, farewell, a promise—it signifies the end—all one's very soul is in one's eyes.

And, in effect, no sooner was my back turned and I stood at my horse's side than all other thoughts left me. I forgot that I had perhaps said a last farewell, in face of the essential importance of assuring myself that nothing of my equipment should be forgotten, that my horse is soundly shod, of tightening up the girths and seeing that my blanket was properly folded, and, automatically, I went on repeating to myself, "Let me see . . . I have my lance, my sword, my carbine, (French cavalry were equipped with the carbine, and not with the infantry rifle as in the case of English). . . . have I thought of everything?" and seemed to look disaster in the face on finding that I had no water-bottle—what was I to do? The very bottle that Flora, the canteen-keeper, had filled with boiling soup in her motherly way—"Oh, my water-bottle"—a real calamity it seemed—empires might crumble; I should have no soup tomorrow morning—all my outlook on war is shrouded in gloom.

Still it was no time to behave like a child. One by one each trooper led his horse into the huge barrack square, where spots of light from electric torches carried by the officers indicated where each troop was to take up its position.

On the chalky ground of the square, showing grey in the darkness, what looked like parallel black lines were growing longer. They were lines of troops, growing into squadrons and increasing until they became the whole regiment. Behind them were the baggage waggons, the travelling forges, machine guns, commandeered carts, the cyclists' detachment and all the rest.

The riding school lay between us and the outer square, which was filled with light and alive with the impatient crowd crushing forward to see us ride out of the narrow way kept open for us, and the time dragged as we waited for every man to be in his place and for the signal to move out.

The horses, impatient at standing still, would paw the ground, and now and again a long-drawn neigh would break the silence. At last a figure appeared in silhouette—it was the colonel.

"Mount!" The two majors repeated the command, and in each half-regiment its two captains, first, then the subalterns and non-commissioned officers repeated it.

A wave seemed to flow from troop to troop like an eddy in a pool, and, sitting rigid in our saddles, our lances held upright, we waited the final order, which was to decide our future and direct us towards the unknown.

"March!" Quitting the dim light of the inner, we came suddenly into the brightly lit outer square, where thousands of hands were held up to bid us a frenzied farewell.

A cry from the crowd followed as we dragoons, sitting like statues, our helmets drawn well down over our faces lest we should betray any sign of emotion, passed out of the barracks which many were never to see again, amid the cheers of a multitude, and the noise of thousands of feet which grew less and less distinct as we rode on.

"I say, old pals, don't forget your sweethearts," cried a little street girl standing on the edge of the foot-path, and that was the last word I heard as Rheims became more and more indistinct in the darkness, whilst we pushed on towards the east.

CHAPTER 2

# After the Germans Had Passed Through

It was on the 6th of August that we crossed the frontier into the Walloon district of Belgium at Muno, to bring succour to the Belgians whose territory had just been violated by the German Army.

In turning over my diary, I select this incident from among many others and stop to describe it, for it seems but right to recall the enthusiastic and touching welcome with which the whole people greeted us—a people now, alas, crushed under the German heel. We were welcomed with open arms—they gave without counting the cost, they threw open their doors to us and could not do enough for the French who had come to join forces with them and bring them succour.

There is not a trooper in my regiment, not a soldier in our whole army, who does not recall that day with feelings of profound emotion.

From the time we left Sedan, our ears still ringing with the cheers that had sent us on our way from Rheims, we received the heartiest of welcomes and good wishes at every village we passed through, but once across the frontier we were acclaimed—prematurely, as it turned out—as veritable conquerors.,

Cavalry on the march, squadron after squadron, has a marked effect on people, and takes the semblance of an invincible rampart against which any enemy must go down.

FRENCH DRAGOONS ON THE MARCH

After seventeen hours in the saddle, with helmet, lance, carbine, sword and full kit, now by a night-time more than disagreeable by reason of an icy cold fog, now under a tropical sun which scorched us, all the while in a cloud of dust, tormented by swarms of midges and horse-flies which hung about us, and tortured by the sight of cherry trees heavy with fruit, which hung over the road, but the branches of which were out of our reach, we approached the frontier.

On the road we passed all the vehicles in the district which had been requisitioned by the military, interminable convoys of them, amongst which, irrespective of class, were humble peasant carts, old-fashioned shaky barouches, motorcars, with the crests of their owners blazoned on the doors, all filled with oats and forage.

Aeroplanes followed us and passed ahead of us flying all-out towards the east. Every now and again we had to draw to the side of the road to allow streams of motor omnibuses drawn from the streets of Paris, filled with *chasseurs* (light infantry), and infantry, to pass by; and our teeth crunched the fine dust that we incessantly breathed.

At length we passed by a fir wood, and a post, painted yellow and black, showed us that we were in Belgium; then we came in sight of a village, almost a hamlet, from which, as we drew near, there rose a noise, the sound of singing, growing louder as we drew near—the *Marseillaise*, sung in welcome by all the folk from the countryside, gathered at their country's gateway to greet us.

All joined in, women, children with shrill voices, even the old men. They ran along after us till we reached the *place*, when the song ceased and a thousand voices cried: "*Vive la France! Vive les Français!*" with such vigour that the horses were startled and cocked their ears in alarm.

One and all brought us gifts, each according to his or her means, fruit, bread, jam, cakes, cigars and cigarettes, pipes and tobacco. I should fill a page with a list of what was thrust upon us. To our parched lips women held flagons of wine or beer, which refreshed us more perhaps when it ran down our cheeks, caked with dust, even than when it found its way down our throats, as the jolting of our horses caused us to spill the precious liquid. It taxed us to stuff away all the dainties in our already overfull pockets, and we stuck cigars into our tunics between the buttons, and flowers in the buttonholes.

A number of French nuns with white head-dresses, like huge white birds, presented us with sacred medallions. I shall always retain graven on my memory the agony depicted in the beautiful, sad eyes of an elderly nun with white hair, who held out to me the last of her collection, a scapular of the Virgin in a brown wrap, and as she did so, said to me, "God guard you, my child."

And in each village, we passed through, that day and the days which followed, we met with the same welcome and the same generosity. It was the same at Basteigné, at Bertrix, at Rochefort, Beauraing, and Ave; indeed everywhere, in the towns as in the villages, the crowd hailed us and fed us. Belgians have handed me boxes of as many as fifty cigarettes.

After exhausting days of twelve or fourteen hours in the saddle I noticed that the troopers, worn out with fatigue, suffering from the heat, from hunger and thirst and intolerable stiffness, sat up in their saddles instinctively as we approached a village, prompted by an unconscious sense of pride in holding up their heads, and I can say, for my part, that such a welcome as we received always banished any feelings of fatigue.

One of our bitterest regrets was having to pass again through Belgium in the reverse direction and to read the dumb surprise on the faces of the people who had thought us unconquerable, but whose great hearts were full only of commiseration for us, worn out as we were, and who, forgetful of their own anxieties, did all in their power to help us.

A peasant woman, I remember, gave us the whole of her provisions, everything that remained in her humble dwelling. The enemy were then advancing on our heels in a threatening wave, and, on my expressing astonishment that she should strip her shelves bare in this fashion, she shook her fist towards the horizon in a fury of rage and exclaimed: "Ah, sir, I prefer that you should eat my provisions rather than leave them a crumb of bread."

Up till the 19th August we had advanced in Belgium; the retreat of the division commenced that same day from Gembloux. We kept on seeking, without success, to get in touch with the German cavalry. Nothing but petty combats took place with insignificant details, a troop at most, but more often with patrols, reconnaissance parties and little groups who surrendered on our approach in a contemptible fashion.

I saw a German major, Prince R——, accompanied by two or three troopers, surrender themselves while still some two hundred metres from one of our weak patrols. They threw down their arms and put up their hands. It was a sickening sight.

Everywhere the enemy's cavalry gave ground, vanished in smoke, became a myth for our regiment, in spite of our forced marches. Each day we spent ten, fifteen, twenty hours in the saddle. One day we actually covered a hundred and thirty kilometres in twenty-two hours, and reached our culminating point to the east, almost under the walls of Liege.

Although we hardly saw any Germans during this first month, we could, *per contra*, follow them by the traces of their crimes.

By day, from village to village, lamentations spread from one horizon to the other, and I regret not having noted the names of the places which were the scenes of the atrocities of which I saw the sequels. I regret not having taken the names of the unhappy women whose children, brothers and husbands had been tortured and shot without motive, not to speak of the outrages which they themselves had undergone, not to speak of the assaults of lechery and Sadism of which they had been the victims. They alluded to these in a fury of rage or made an involuntary confession in an agony of humiliation and grief.

By night a furrow of fire traced the enemy's path. The Germans burnt everything that was susceptible of being burnt— ricks, barns, farms, entire villages, which blazed like torches, lighting the countryside with a weird light.

We entered villages of which nothing remained except smoking and calcined stones, before which families, who had lost their all, grieved and wrung their powerless hands at the sight of some black debris which had once been all their joy, their hearth and home.

I wish particularly to insist that these deeds were not the result of *accident*, for we were daily witnesses of them for a whole month. I still shiver when I think of the confidences which I have received. The pen may not write down all the facts, all the abominations, all the hateful things, all the lowest and most degrading filthiness inspired by the imagination of crazy erotomaniacs. It was always Sadism which seemed to guide their acts and predominate amongst their misdeeds.

Here a mother mourned a child, shot for some childish prank; there a young girl grieved for her *fiancé*, hung because he was of military age; farther on a helpless old man had had his house pillaged and had been brutally treated because he had nothing else to offer. At every step we heard the story of crime, and those guilty deserve to be hung. Such are the things of which such an enemy was capable—an enemy who refused combat, who advanced hastily under cover of night to rob and burn a defenceless village, and who seemed to vanish like smoke at the approach of our troops, leaving in our hands hardly more than some drunken stragglers unable to regain their army, or some robbers who had waited behind to rob a house or to violate a woman, and had been taken in the act.

We passed through all that in our endless quest, always in the saddle, sleeping two or three hours at night, in an exasperating search for the German cavalry, which was constantly reported to be within gun-shot, but which disappeared by enchantment each time we approached. To give an idea of what we endured, I have transcribed word for word the notes from my field pocket-book describing some of these August days. These notes were written in most cases on horseback by the roadside during a halt.

*7th August.*—Torrential rain; twelve hours in the saddle; we are worn out with fatigue; put up at Basteigné; arrived at night. My troop is on guard. I mount duty at the bridge; we are fed by the populace, nothing to eat from rations.

*8th August,*—*Réveillé* 3 o'clock, mounted a last turn of duty at the bridge till 5 o'clock. Departure; rested at midday in an open field for dinner. While we are eating, enemy is reported near; we follow immediately towards Liége. Don't come up with them. March at night till one in the morning; have done one hundred and thirty kilometres and twenty hours on horseback, sleep in an open field from two to four.

*9th August,*—Torrid heat, men and horses done up; billeted at Ave after twelve hours in the saddle. First squadron ambushed. Lieutenant Chauvenet killed. The Germans flee, burning the villages, killing women and children.

*11th August,*—Leave Ave at 5 o'clock. The heat appears to increase, not a breath of air. For two hours we trot in clouds of blinding dust. A regiment of *Uhlans* is reported. The colonel masses us behind a hill and we think we are going to deliver battle; but the enemy steals away once more. Thirst is a torture, my water-bottle lasts no time. Arrive at Beauraing at six o'clock. Thirteen hours in the saddle.

*12th August,*—We onsaddled at 5 o'clock. False alarm; wait at Beauraing.

*14th August,*—Alarm, the regiment moves off; I am left behind to accompany a convoy of reservists. The village is barricaded, the enemy is quite near. Only a handful of men are with the convoy. Wait at the side of the road with Fuéminville and Lubeké. Five dismounted men arrive, without helmets, done up, limping, prostrated, grim as those who have seen a sight which will for ever prevent them from smiling; the fact is that the remains of the 3rd squadron of the 16th have been caught in an ambush by the German infantry concealed in a wood. They have been shot down at point-blank range without being able to put up a fight.

Never have I seen human waifs more lamentable and more tragic. They had seen all their comrades fall at their side and owed their lives only to the fact that they had themselves fallen under their dead horses and to a flight of 40 kilometres through the woods. Montcalm is amongst the killed. The convoy marched out at half-past nine at night, at the walk, an exasperating pace of 4 kilometres an hour. We took all night to do 23 kilometres. I ask myself when we are likely to rejoin the 22nd, even whether the 22nd still exists.

*15th August.*—We bivouac near the village of Authée, with the convoys of the 61st and 5th Chasseurs. It is dark and cold, and this night has tired me more than my longest marches. The waiting about unnerves us, and my blood boils when I think that the 22nd must be on the eve of having a fight. The Germans lay siege to Dinant eight kilometres off. One hears the guns as if they were alongside. Our turn is near, I think. No one is affected thereby, and we prepare our soup to the whistling of shells. The cannonade seems to redouble, they are giving and taking hard knocks, and some there will be who won't answer their names tonight.

*Ten o'clock,*—The different convoys move off. 16th, 22nd, 9th, 28th, 32nd Dragoons, etc. All at once we are stupefied by seeing a battalion of the 33rd of the line, or rather what remains of the battalion, some thirty terrifying beings, livid, stumbling along, with horrible wounds. One has his lips carried away, an officer has a crushed hand, another has his arm fractured by a shell splinter. Their uniforms are torn, white with dust and drip with blood. Amongst the last comers the wounds are more villainous; in the waggons one sees bare legs that hang limp, bloodless faces. They come from Dinant, where the French have fought like lions. Our artillery arrived too late, but they had the fine courage to charge the German guns with the bayonet. The guns spit shell without cease and the crackle of musketry does not stop.

We go across country to billet at Florennes. These last days of tropical heat give place to damp cold. It is raining. We meet long convoys of inhabitants who, panic-stricken, quit their houses to go and camp anywhere at all. It is lamentable. Two kilometres from Florennes we "incline." The cold is biting, in spite of the cloak I wear. We arrive in black darkness at a village where we bivouac in spite of the torrential rain. I rejoin the regiment with infinite trouble; clothes, kit, horses are dripping wet. They must

A DRAGOON COLUMN IN THE RAIN

stay so all night. I do a stable guard at three in the morning without a lantern. The horses are tied up by groups to a horseshoe. They kick and rear, upsetting the kit and the lances in the mud; I dabble about and lose myself in the night. The village is called Biesmérée.

*Sunday, 16th August,*—The weather has cleared up. I leave again with the regiment. We are going to put up at Maisons-Saint-Gérard. Just before arriving there a storm bursts and wets us through; the water runs down into our breeches. I am as wet as if I had been dipped in a river; and one must sleep like that . . . . . and yet one does not die!

*17th August,*—Off at 5 o'clock. We bivouac at Saint-Martin in the meadow between two small streams. I have hurt my left foot badly, and at times I feel an overpowering fatigue, but one must carry on all the same. The bivouac is admirable. Big fires warm up the soup for the troops. The little stream shimmers, all red, and encircles the bivouac. The day ends; splendid. . . . .Some *cuirassiers* bivouac a little higher up on the village green. We hear them singing the *Marseillaise.* We sleep in a barn in heaps one on the top of the other.

*19th August,*—The 4th squadron is on reconnaissance. We start alone, at a venture. We are in the saddle all day. At night we make a triumphal entry into Gembloux and we are baited with drinks and food. The Germans are at the gates of the town and the crowd is wildly excited. The sun goes down without a cloud, round as a wafer. I forget the day's fatigues and we venture across the plain and the woods. It is an agonising moment; we hide ourselves behind a long rick of flax; the enemy is some hundreds of metres off and all night we have sentries out. I slept two hours yesterday, today I am passing the whole night on foot. The cold is cruel. Now and then my legs give way and I nearly fall on my knees. We have had nothing to eat but bread, the chill damp gets into our bones. Some Taubes pass, sowing agony.

*20th August.*—I am one of the point party under Lieutenant Chatelin. We fire on some horsemen at 600 metres. The squad-

31

ron is still on reconnaissance. One could sit down and cry from fatigue. We advance towards Charleroi, whose approaches are several kilometres long. A population of miners. Everywhere are foundries, mines, factories, and for two hours unceasing acclamation. We arrive at a suburb of Charleroi, done up, falling out of our saddles. Interminable wait on the *place*; night falls. The camp kit comes up at last, but the march is not yet over, we are camping five kilometres farther on. It is enough to kill one. We get to Landelies. Rest at last, we bivouac. I share a bed, with Delettrez, for the first time for three weeks. In a bed at one side a fat old woman is sleeping. No matter, it is an unforgettable night.

*21st August.*—Landelies; rest; we satisfy our hunger; we expect to pass a quiet day and night. At four o'clock we are off to an alarm; we are in the saddle all night and arrive in a little village, whose name I forget, half dead with hunger and cold. The peasants give us bread. We have been all day on horseback.

*22nd August,*—Are we going to have a little rest? No, we were out of bed all night and we are at it again. We do not understand the movements we are carrying out. *Are we retreating?* The fatigue is becoming insupportable. We get to Bousignies at three in the morning. On the road I lost my horse during a halt and I found myself alone in the night and on foot. I had all the trouble in the world to catch up the squadron on foot. We slept two hours in the rain in a field of beetroot. Off again at 9 o'clock. Loud firing twenty kilometres off. All the peasants are clearing out. They say that Charleroi is on fire.

And so it goes on each day till the end of the month. The 26th we marched in the direction of Cambrai; we put up at Epehy, which the enemy burnt the following day. The peasants replied by themselves setting fire to the crops to prevent their falling into the enemies' hands.

At Roisel, a whole train of goods blazed in the midday heat. We went on to Péronne. The 28th we were at Villers-Carbonel, where I was present at an unforgettable artillery combat. I saw shells throw some French skirmishers in the air by groups of three and four at a time. We left Villers-Carbonel in flames, and, from that moment, we beat a rapid retreat towards Paris, passing by Sourdon, Maisoncelle, Beauvais, Villers-sur-Thère, Breançon, Meulan, Les Alluets-le-Roi, and, after a last and painful stage, we put up at Loges-en-Josas, four kilometres from Versailles, where the fortune of war brought me to one of our own estates. Thus, it came about that my mother, who believed me to be at the other end of Belgium, caught sight of me one fine morning coming up the central drive to the *château* on foot, leading my horse, my lance on my shoulder, followed by a long file of troopers.

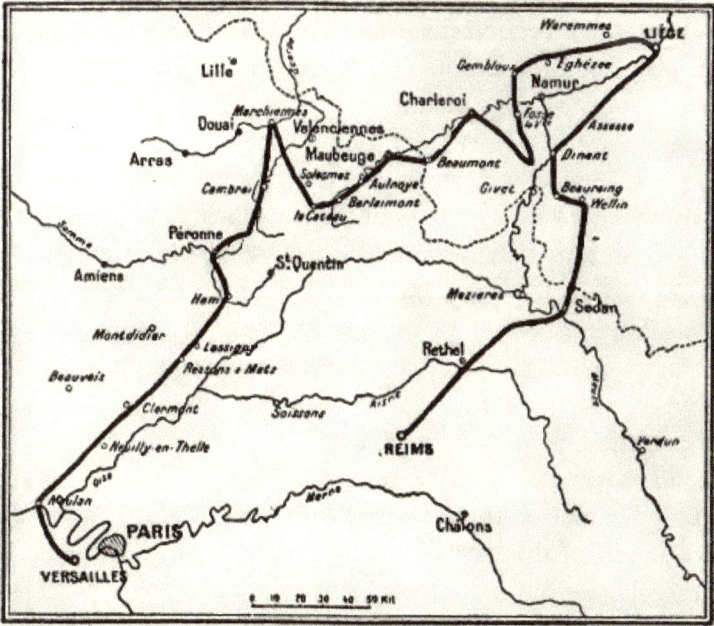

MAP ILLUSTRATING THE ROUTE FOLLOWED BY THE 22ND REGIMENT OF DRAGOONS.

## Chapter 3

# The Escape in the Forest of Compiègne

6TH TO 10TH SEPTEMBER, 1914

Having left Versailles, we arrived at Saint-Mard on the 6th of September to find ourselves in the thick of the Battle of the Marne. The struggle extended all around us, from one horizon to the other, and if it was incomprehensible to our officers it was still more so to us private soldiers. In the evening, from Loges-en-Josas, where we had been billeted, we heard the guns. Every-one was sure that Paris would be invested within the next two days, and then we were suddenly sent off to be stranded some forty kilometres to the north-east of Paris. We were ignorant of the movements going on, and we were amazed and quite out of our reckoning, hardly daring to believe that the enemy, who the evening before was thought to be at the gates of Paris, was now in retreat.

For my own part I preserve only a confused and burning recollection of the days of the 6th and 7th of September, days memorable amongst all others, since they saw the beginning of the victorious offensive of the armies of Maunoury, of Foch, of French and of Langle de Cary. The heat was suffocating. The exhausted men, covered with a layer of black dust adherent from sweat, looked like devils. The tired horses, no longer off-saddled, had large open sores on their backs. The air was burning; thirst was intolerable, and there was no possibility of procuring a drop of water. All around us the guns thundered. The horizon was, as it were, encircled with a moving line of bursting shells, and we knew nothing, absolutely nothing.

In the torrid midday heat we kept advancing, without knowing where or why. We passed a disturbed night rolled in our cloaks in an open field, without rations and already suffering from hunger. The next day was a repetition of the last and was passed in the same hateful state of physical exhaustion and of moral inquietude. From time to time, behind some hill, beyond some wood, quite near, a sudden and violent musketry fire broke out; the gun fire redoubled in intensity and we heard the whistle of the shrapnel passing high over us, and the noise of the bursting shell. There, we said to ourselves, is the fighting; there, no, there, and then there on the left, on the right; it was everywhere.

Repeatedly our column had to make sudden detours to avoid artillery fire. Still we knew nothing, and we continued our march as in a dream, under the scorching sun, gnawed by hunger, parched with thirst and so exhausted by fatigue that I could see my comrades stiffen themselves in the saddle to prevent themselves from falling. The sun went down with a splendour that no one thought of admiring. Little by little, insensibly, our figures bent forward till they touched the wallets on our saddles, and we gave way to a sort of torpor. Then a long tremor ran along the ranks.

Above the village of Troène we fell into the thick of the fight. This happened so quickly that I preserve only a visual image of it. We had slowly climbed a hill, whose shadow concealed the setting sun from us. As we came out on the crest of the hill, we caught a sudden glimpse of a regiment of *Chasseurs-à-Cheval*, silhouetted in black against the immense red screen of the sky, charging like a whirlwind, with drawn sabres.

A "75" gun on our flank fired without interruption. I can see now a wounded *chasseur* who rose from the grass where he lay almost under the muzzle of the gun, and who fell back, as if struck by lightning, from the displacement of air caused by the shell. A second later nothing was to be seen except a confused *mêlée* behind a small wood. The noise was terrible, and was made up of a thousand different sounds. An officer of *chasseurs*, with a bullet through his chest, bareheaded, all splashed with blood, came down the hill leaning on his sword, and leaving behind him a long trail which reddened the grass. Then the sun seemed to perish as the immense uproar died down; all the noises died away, and we continued our road in the rapidly falling darkness, having had a sudden and fugitive vision of one scene amongst the thousands which compose the drama of a great battle.

All night we had marched without repose, without food. In our exhaustion we had become the spectres of our former selves, and our hearts were breaking from discouragement. We did not know that right alongside of us the most victorious offensive in the history of the world was commencing. We did not suspect that, under pressure from General Maunoury, the German 4th Reserve Corps was giving way, and that this must assure the rout and the final defeat of Von Kluck's army.

From the 8th we began to play an active part in the great battle. The 5th Cavalry Division was ordered to surprise a German convoy and to seize it. The officers told us of this mission. At last we were going to do something; our time of waiting was at an end, and there was to be no more wandering about the burnt-up country, devoured by thirst and discouraged at feeling ourselves lost and forgotten in the great struggle we had set our hand to. The convoy would be four kilometres long, and we could already imagine the attack, the taking of the booty. It was going to be a romantic and amusing episode, and the dragoons sat up in their saddles, forgetting their fatigue and their hunger, and full of joy at the thought of the promised combat.

In my inner self I could not share the general enthusiasm; I felt that we had been exactly marked down by the enemy's aircraft which flew over us each moment, insolently bidding defiance to our rifle and machine-gun fire.

The expedition, however, started off well. A young dragoon, sent forward as scout, penetrated into a farm and there found fifteen Prussian staff officers engaged in stuffing themselves with food. He calmly pointed his revolver at them and advised them to surrender. "My regiment will be here directly; any resistance is useless." In reality he had to keep them under the muzzle of

GUERRE 1914-1915. — Spahis Marocains traversant la rorêt de Compiègne.
Morrocan Spahis passing through the Forest of Compiègne. — LL.

Visé Paris n° 90

his revolver for a long quarter of an hour, for the regiment was still far off. A major having shown signs of moving, the dragoon blew out his brains at point-blank range, and he succeeded in keeping them all terrorised until our arrival. This capture stimulated still further the general good humour.

I can still see six of the fourteen prisoners file past the flank of the column, each between two dragoons, a forage cord tied to the reins of their horses, and I can see again the cunning and furious look of a *"hauptmann"* still bloated with the feast which we had prevented him from completing. I remember the gay, frank laugh of the whole regiment, its light-heartedness at having laid hands on these fat eaters of *choucroute*, who were too astonished even to be insolent.

A few moments afterwards three German motorcars were sighted three hundred metres off, going at a prudent pace. At once the ranks were broken and we galloped furiously at them, each straining hard to be the first to get there; but, by quickly reversing their engines, the three chauffeurs succeeded in turning and made off at top speed, riddled by machine-gun fire, but out of range for us. The last of them, however, was destined to fall into our hands next morning, having been damaged by a shot in its petrol tank. We had to set it on fire so as not to abandon it to the enemy, who were pressing us on all sides. Half my regiment was now detached from the division and charged with the task of capturing, unaided, the tail of a convoy which was reputed to have broken down on the road.

At nightfall we entered the forest of Villers-Cotterets, under the command of Major Jouillié, and I was assailed by an acute presentiment of misfortune. I parted from the other half of the regiment and from the other regiments of the division with the clear and irresistible intuition that I would not see them again for a long time, and shortly afterwards we melted like shadows under the trees of the great dark forest.

Then commenced, for me, one of the most painful episodes of the whole war. The silence of the forest was lugubrious. A Taube persisted in flying over us, quite near to the ground, like a great blackbird. Its shadow grazed us, one might have said, and nothing was more harassing and more demoralising than this enemy that followed us and kept persistently on our track. At cross-roads, as we came out into a large clearing, it let fall three long coloured smoke balls to signal our presence to its artillery, which was doubtless quite near but of whose position we were ignorant. Then it disappeared with a rapid flight, and the night fell black as ink around us.

The voices of the officers seemed grave. The continual thrusts which the column made, its returns on its tracks, gave me to understand that we were groping our way, not knowing which to take. We descended in double file a terribly steep narrow path, preceded by the machine-guns, which had only just room enough to pass. The soft soil sunk in like a marsh. Then there was a sudden halt and, quite near me, I saw the major's face, full of anxiety. Addressing Captain de Tarragon in a choking voice he said, "The machine-guns are done for." The rest of the phrase was lost, but I heard the words "bogged, engulfed, impossible to get them out...."

We were ordered to incline, and we climbed up again to the forest. All the men were alarmed at the loss of the machine-guns, abandoned in the marsh, and the face of Desoil, the non-commissioned officer with the machine-guns, was heart-breaking. His mouth worked but no words came.

With this discouragement all of us felt a renewal of hunger which was painfully acute. Thirst too burnt our throats, and fatigue weighed down our exhausted limbs. Ah, how I envied the horses which nibbled the leaves and the grass. For two days our water-bottles had been empty, we had already finished our reserve rations and this contributed to the gloom on our faces.

Towards midnight, the village of Bonneuil-en-Valois was vaguely outlined in the night at the edge of the forest. The hungry and tired horses stumbled at each step; almost all the men were dozing on their wallets, and we committed the irreparable fault of dismounting and of sleeping heavily on the open ground, instead of utilising the cover of night to join one of the neighbouring divisions by a forced march. A small post composed of a corporal and four men was the only guard for our

French dragoons with German prisoners

bivouac. Each of us had passed his horse's reins under his arm, and all of us slept, officers and men alike, like tired brutes. We did not suspect that our sentinels were posted hardly three hundred metres from the German sentries, who were concealed from us by a fold in the ground which held a regiment of Prussian infantry, who had chanced to get there, within rifle range, just at the same time as we.

At dawn a neighing horse, some clash of arms, probably gave away our position, and the alarm was given in the enemy's camp, which was separated from us only by a field of standing lucerne. The troopers slept on, and the German scouts crept up, absolutely invisible.

A sudden musketry fire woke us up, and the German infantry was on us. I cannot think of these moments without giving credit to the admirable presence of mind which saved the situation by the avoidance of all panic. The horses were not girthed up, many of the kits had slipped round, reins were unbuckled; no matter, we had to mount. I have a crazy recollection of my loose girth, of my saddle slipping round, of the blanket which had worked forward on to my horse's neck; no matter, "Forward! Forward!" a second's delay might be our ruin.

A hail of bullets fell amongst us. Alongside of me, Alaire, a quite young non-commissioned officer, was hit in the belly. He was the first in the regiment whom I had seen fall. God! what a horrible toss he took, dragged by his horse, maddened by fear, crying out, "Rolland, Rolland, don't abandon me." Then, in a last contortion, his foot came out of the stirrup and he died convulsed by a final spasm. Near me, the captain's orderly gave a loud shout; horses, mortally wounded, galloped wildly for some metres and then suddenly fell as if pole-axed.

I saw a man who, as if seized with madness, sent his wounded horse headlong to the bottom of a ravine and then threw himself after.

"Forward! Forward!" I followed the others, who made off towards the village. My horse trod on a German whose throat, gashed by a lance thrust, poured out such a stream of blood that the earth under me was red and streaming with it. "Forward! Forward!"

We were not going to view them then, these enemies who killed us without our seeing them, so hidden were they amongst the grass that they blended with the soil? Yes, we were though, and suddenly surprise stopped short the rush of the squadrons. Before us, some metres off, and so near that we could almost touch it with our lances, an aeroplane got up, like a partridge surprised in a stubble. A cry of rage burst from every throat. We tried to charge it with our lances in the air, but it mocked our efforts, and our rearing horses were on the spot ten seconds too late. The enemy seemed also to have flown. All that remained were two or three grey corpses that strewed the soil. We trotted into the village with our heads down, humiliated at having been fooled like children.

After having passed the first few isolated farms along our road, an enemy's section came for us, exposing themselves entirely this time, while a line of recumbent skirmishers fired a volley into us from our right, almost at point-blank range. There was nothing for it but to retire, unless we wanted to remain there as dead men, and at the gallop, the more so because a machine-gun was riddling the walls of a farm with little black points. We passed before it like a whirlwind; and, happily, its murderous fire was too high to hit us. I can still recall the sight of an isolated German, caught between the fire of his regiment and the charge of our horses. I turned my head and laughed with joy at seeing a comrade pierce him with his lance in passing.

The Germans were all round us, and our only line of retreat was by the forest, into which we all plunged in a common rush without waiting for orders. The forest, at least, represented safety for the moment. It was a sanctuary calculated to protect us from an entire army, until we died of hunger. For a long time we marched in silence, cutting across the wood, avoiding the beaten path, for our intention was to attain the very heart of the forest, or some impenetrable spot where we could not be discovered, where we could regain our breath and where our officers could deliberate and take a decision. The whole half-regiment took shelter at last in an immense ravine, where we were sheltered from aircraft. We were covered by a thick vault of leaves in a sort of prehistoric gorge, which seemed far from all civilisation and lost in an ocean of verdure, and there we dismounted. The major sent patrols to explore the issues from the forest, and we waited some mortal hours without daring to raise our voices.

Our situation was almost desperate. For three days we had touched not a morsel of bread, not a biscuit, our horses not a handful of corn. The reserve rations were exhausted; and the patrols, which came in one after the other, brought sad news. The Germans were masters of all the issues from the forest, and we were taken in a vice, prisoners in this gulf of trees and reduced to dying of hunger and thirst. A little way off, the officers—Major Jouillié, Captain de Salverte, Captain de Tarragon, Monsieurs Chatelin, Cambacérés, Roy and de Thézy—deliberated with glum faces.

Each stood near his horse so as to be able to jump on in case of surprise. In spite of everything the men's spirits remained admirable. All had a jest on their lips, and the more serious amongst them wrote a line to their wives or mothers. Leaning against the trunk of a tree, I scribbled on two letter-cards, found in my wallets, two short notes of *adieu*. The day passed with depressing slowness.

Towards four o'clock two officers of *Uhlans* appeared on a little road which, so to speak, hung above us. At once all eyes were fixed on these two thin silhouettes. They advanced, talking quietly, with their reins loose on their horses' necks. How great was the temptation to shoulder one's carbine, take steady aim, feel one's man at the end of the muzzle and kill him dead with a ball through the heart! Everyone understood, however, that it was necessary to keep quiet and let off the prey so good a mark was it, for doing so would have given the alarm and signalised our presence. Now they were right on us, so near that we could have touched them, and yet they did not know that there were two hundred carbines which could have knocked them over at point-blank range.

Even now I can distinctly see the face of the first, as if it were photographed on my brain. He was quite young, with an eye-glass well screwed into the eye, his face was red and insolent, just

as the Prussian officer is always represented. He had a whip under his arm, and he even had a cigar. Suddenly his face and that
of his companion contracted, as if confronted by some appari-
tion. This French regiment must have seemed to them a phan-
tom of the forest, some impossible and illusory vision seen in
the shadow of the leaves. Their horses stopped short and, for the
space of a second, their riders looked like two figures in stone.
Then in a flash they understood and fled at full speed. For an
instant we heard the stones fly under their horses' shoes, but the
sound grew fainter and fainter, and a deep silence reigned again.

The alarm had been given, the danger had still further increased, and, now that our place of concealment had been discovered, we had to start off again across the thicket and rock on
our poor done-up horses. On reflecting over it, my mind refuses
to believe that such a cross-country ride was possible. To throw
the enemy off the scent it was necessary to pass where no one
would have imagined that a horse could go, and that involved
a ride into the abyss in the deepening night, plunges into black
gulfs, intersected by trunks of trees, to the foot of which some
horsemen and their horses rolled like broken toys.

I felt my old horse, Teint, curl up and tremble between my
legs. His hair stood on end and his nostrils opened and shut. On,
on, ever on . . . to the very heart of the old forest, whose most se-
cret solitudes we troubled, frightening the herds of deer, which
fled terrified before our cavalcade. For a moment it seemed as
if we were at some monstrous hunt on horseback with men for
quarry, and in spite of myself, a mortal fatigue seized on me. I
shut my eyes and waited for the "Gone away." Better it were to
be finished quickly, since the game was lost.

The troops had got mixed and I found myself again for a
moment amongst the 3rd squadron by the side of Lieutenant
Cambacérés, and we exchanged a few brief words. Almost tim-
idly, so absurd did the idea appear that one of us could escape,
I asked him to write a line home if it were my luck to be done
for and if he came out safe. I promised him the same service, if
the roles were reversed. To such an extent does gaiety enter into
the composition of our French nature, we even joked for a few

moments and we shared a last tablet of chocolate, which he had preserved in his wallets, a service for which I shall always be grateful to him, for hunger was causing me insupportable pain.

We were now going at a slow pace over a carpet of dead leaves, amongst trees which were singularly thinned out. Our object being to gain the heart of the forest, we had ended up by reaching its border, and we remained glued to the spot, holding our breath at the sudden vision seen through the branches.

The famous convoys that the division was out to take were there, in front of us, on a stretch of some eight kilometres of road. Waggons of munitions, provision carts, watercarts, lorries of all sorts, were moving gaily along at an easy walk, and the rumbling noise was continuous.

In the calm of the evening each spoken word, each order given by the guides came to us clear and distinct. Then came the last vehicles, the last country carts, some stragglers tailing out into a confusion of cyclists and horsemen; and so, the interminable convoy went on its way. The vehicles at its head had the appearance of toys on the horizon, of toys designed with the pen on the gold of the sky; and the personnel looked like insects finely traced in the clear atmosphere.

The whole thing went quietly on its way like a slow caravan. One would have said that here was a people coming to settle in conquered country and arriving at the end of its journey in the peace of a lovely evening. The same day, at the same moment, General Foch, pushing the thin end of his wedge between the armies of Bülow and those of Hausen, enlarged that fissure which was to prove fatal to the German Army which had almost arrived at the Marne. The pursuit was about to begin. These same convoys, whose peaceful aspect wounded our hearts from the insolence of their air of possession on French soil (we were ignorant of course that the dawn of a great victory was about to break)—these same convoys, lashed by terror and by the breath of panic, were going to follow beaten armies in a headlong and wild retreat, leaving on the road their waggons and stores.

From this moment a vague hope sprang up in our hearts and, as is often the case, we gathered courage when the worst of catastrophes seemed to be heaping on our heads.

Night fell little by little. It was impossible to remain where we were. We were well within the German lines, of this there was no doubt, since we had the enemy's troops behind us, while their convoys were on in front of us; but, under cover of night we might attempt a desperate stroke, and anything was better than dying of hunger. Towards ten at night our column came bravely out of the forest—a silent column whose members looked like phantoms. Cutting across country, we avoided Haramont, Eméville, Bonneuil-en-Valois, Morienval.

As night fell a sombre gloom seized on us. All those silent villages, which we dared not approach, had a threatening appearance; lights appeared suddenly, more or less distant; a succession of luminous points was moving slowly, like a moving train going slowly. I was ill at ease, and this was causing me physical pain; my saddle girth was too loose and had allowed my horse's blanket to slip till it threatened to fall off. No matter, for nothing in the world would I dismount. It seemed as if hands came out of the shadows and stretched forth to seize me.

A breath of superstitious terror blew over us, and, in the deep surrounding silence, a single persistent and regular noise made us start with the fear of the unknown. It was the screech of the owl, an unnatural cry which seemed like a signal replied to in the distance; and it made us shudder. My eyes eagerly searched the shadow to discover a hidden enemy. Twice I could have sworn that I saw a group of German uniforms, two mounted *Uhlans*, another on foot; but I mistrusted my eyes, hallucinations being of common occurrence at night, and I tried to pluck up courage.

While crossing a road a sudden noise and a cry of "Help!" rang out, a cry choked with agony and terror. It came from one of our men, whose horse had struck into mine and had rolled into the ditch. I turned and saw in a flash a brief struggle which the night at once blotted out. This time I had made no mistake. There really were two Germans struggling with our comrade; but I was carried on by the forward movement, and profound silence reigned again. If we were surrounded by enemies, why this conspiracy of silence? The horrid screech of the owl never ceased, imparting panic to our disordered imaginations, making us think that even a catastrophe was preferable to this maddening incertitude, to this agony of doubt. During this time, I lived the worst hours of my life.

We advanced, however, marching from west to east, and soon we entered the great black mass of the forest of Compiègne, from whence arose four or five bird-calls as we approached. No matter; for the second time the forest represented safety for us, and imder the impenetrable shade of its tall trees we followed its edge in the direction of Champlieu, sometimes followed, sometimes preceded by the hooting which announced, as we learnt later, our approach and our passage.

At the moment when our agony was at an end, when hope revived, when, even, certain men giving way to fatigue had bent down on to their wallets drunk with sleep—at that moment we fell definitely into the mousetrap into which the Germans had methodically decoyed us, and a desperate attack was made on us from all sides. The drama took place so rapidly that I can remember only detached shreds of it. The clouds parted, letting fall a flood of moonlight; somewhere a cry resounded in the night, and the black forest seemed to spit fire. Thousands of brief flashes lit up each thicket, a hail of bullets thinned the column, and mingled with this were cries and a terrible neighing from the horses, some of which reared, while others lay kicking on the ground, dragging their riders and their kits in a spasm of terrible agony.

Instinctively each trooper made a "left turn" and galloped furiously to get out of range of this murderous fire which decimated our ranks. In a few seconds we had put two hundred metres between the forest and us, and the two squadrons rallied under cover of a slight mist.

As we rode a squadron sergeant-major, Dangel, gave a groan, as his horse carried him off after the others. Then I saw him collapse, pitch forward on his nose on to his horse's fore shoulder and fall to the ground, to be dragged. I leapt from my horse and managed to disengage his foot. Holding him in my arms, I begged him to show a little pluck.

"We must clear out of this or we will be taken prisoners. For God's sake get on your horse."

His only response was a long sigh, then his heavy body collapsed in my arms, and he dragged me to the ground. For a second I was perplexed. The others were far off, and I alone remained behind with a dying man in my arms, who clasped me in desperate embrace. At last his arms let go, and a spasm stretched him dead at my feet. I laid him piously on the grass with his face to the sky, and when I had finished this last duty to a comrade, I raised my head and saw a whole line of skirmishers fifty metres off. For a moment a feeling possessed me that I could not get away; but, damn, they were not going to take me alive. An extraordinary calm came over me.

I remounted slowly, made sure that I had picked up all four reins and lowered my lance. Now, by the grace of God . . . now for it. A volley greeted my departure, but it was written that I was to escape. Several bullets grazed me, not one hit me. Soon I was out of range and concealed by a curtain of fog. I rejoined the two squadrons, many of whose troopers were without horses. Two hundred metres farther on a fresh fusillade came from the invisible trenches and decimated our already thinned ranks. Captain de Tarragon, whose horse had been wounded, pitched forward and remained pinned under his horse. I passed by him at the gallop hardly seeing him, and I heard a shout that seemed to illumine the very darkness: "Charge, my lads." This shout, repeated by all, swelled, increased and became a savage clamour, which must have paralysed the enemy, for the fusillade ceased and cries of "Wer da" were heard at different points.

Afterwards I shut my eyes and tried to remember, but for some moments everything was mixed up. I recall a furious gallop at the dark holes where the Germans had gone to earth. A high trench embankment faced us and my horse got to the other side after a monstrous scramble. Before me and on my right and left I saw horses taking complete somersaults; I could not say whether it lasted a minute or an hour. The pains and the privations of the last three days culminated in a moment of madness. We had

UHLANS ROUTED BY FRENCH DRAGOONS.

to get through, cost what it might; we had to bowl over every-thing, break through everything, but get through all the same, and our hot and furious gallop grew faster under the heedless moon, which bathed the country with its pale and gentle light. Three times we charged, three times we charged down on the obstacle without knowing its nature, until the remains of the two squadrons found themselves, breathless, in a little depression at the edge of a wood, before an impassable wall of barbed wire.

Impatient voices shouted for wire-cutters, and during the delay before these were forthcoming, a few panic-mongers blurted out false news, which soon circulated and which all believed: "The enemy is advancing in skirmishing order." "We are going to be shot down at point-blank range," etc. . . . Had the news been true, I would not have given much for our skins. Huddled together like a flock of sheep before the gap which some of our men were exerting themselves to open up for our passage, a handful of resolute infantry could have killed every one of us.

At last the gap was made and I descended a steep slope between the thin stems of the birches, having been sent forward as scout by my major, whom I was never to see again. Below, a figure in silhouette and bareheaded was resting on his sword in the middle of a clearing bathed in moonlight. He watched me coming, and I was astonished to recognise in him the officer of my troop. For a brief moment each had taken the other for an enemy, and at twenty metres off we were each ready to fall on the other. Our mutual recognition was none the less cordial.

M. Chatelin refused my horse, which I offered to him, deciding to try to regain our lines on foot under cover of night (which he did after having knocked over two German sentries). He warned me expressly against some skirmishers concealed in a thicket behind me, and after a hearty handshake and a "good luck," which sounded supremely ironical between two such isolated individuals, lost in the heart of German "territory," I watched his thin silhouette melt into the darkness.

I made my way back to give an account of my mission and to tell the major that this route was impracticable for the two squadrons. Above, the plain extended to infinity, white in the moonlight, with no vestige of a human being! All that was to be seen were two horses which galloped wildly to an accompaniment of clashing stirrups, and the uneasy neighs of lost animals—that whinny of the horse which has something so human in it gave me a shudder. How was it that two squadrons had had the time, during my brief absence, to melt and disappear?

What road have they found? Why have they abandoned me? The terror of desolation took the place of my former calm. To die with the others in the midst of a charge would have been fine; but to feel oneself lost and alone in all this mystery, in this endless night, in the midst of thousands of invisible enemies, was a bit too much. It was a childish nightmare and, seized with the same panic as the lost horses, I too spurred mine till his flanks bled, and I set off straight before me galloping like a madman. Luck, or perhaps my horse who scented his stable companions, brought me all at once to a small contingent of dragoons—Captain de Salverte and eleven men, with whom I joined up. I questioned the captain, who could tell me nothing.

He had found himself detached and lost like me, and he had put himself at our head to try to get us out of this inextricable position. We walked on gloomily through a country cut up by hedges and streams. Shortly, we found ourselves within a few metres of an enemy's bivouac, the fires of which made the shadows dance on our drawn faces. A stupid sentry was warming himself, and had his back turned to us. What was the good of struggling? Why cheat oneself with chimerical illusions? The day would dawn and we would be ingloriously surprised and sent to some prisoner's camp in the centre of Germany, unless, choosing to die rather than yield, we kept for ourselves the last shot in our magazines.

However, we reached the forest. In the maze of dark paths, we lost the Captain and Sergeant Pathé. With Farrier Sergeant-Major Delfour, and Sergeant-Major Desoil of the machine-gun section, nine of us were left, and we were determined to try a last effort, spurred by an awakening of that instinct of self-preservation which stiffens the desire to live in the very face of death.

Deep in the forest we passed the night concealed in a thicket, taking pity on our horses, which would have died had we demanded a further effort of them. Soon we were overpowered by sleep, sleep so profound that the entire German army might have surprised us, without our raising a little finger to get away. At daybreak we continued our way, with stiff and benumbed limbs and soaking clothing. It was a beautiful autumn day. Wisps of pink mist wrapped to the tree tops.

A large stag watched our coming with uneasy surprise, standing in the middle of a paved road on his slim legs. He disappeared with a bound into a clump of bushes, whose swaying branches let fall a shower of silver drops. A divine peace possessed all space. In a clearing some thirty loose horses had got together. The larger number were saddled and carried the complete equipment of regiments of dragoons and of *chasseurs*. The lances lay on the ground, together with complete sets of kit and mess tins.

Surely the enemy had not passed this way or he would have laid hands on all this material so hurriedly abandoned; and yet no human being was about who could tell us anything, not even a lost soldier. There was no one but ourselves and the immense tranquil forest, gilded by early autumn, splashed with the dark green of the oaks and with every shade of colour from ardent purple to the white leaf of the aspen.

That glorious dawn shone on the greatest victory the world had ever seen. The battle was over for the armies of Maunoury, of French, of Franchet, of d'Estrey, of Foch, and of Langle de Gary. The pursuit was beginning, and the whole extent of country, where we were now wandering, pursued and tracked like wild beasts, was going to be cleared within a few hours of the last German who had sullied its soil.

More than thrice during the morning we came unexpectedly on German detachments, isolated parties, lost patrols or stragglers, and each time we cut across the wood to escape them at the risk of breaking our necks. Then we got to a long straight path at the lower end of which a fine limousine motorcar had been abandoned, and at the end of the path we reached a village which appeared to be empty. We consulted together for a moment, being in doubt what to do; but all of us were loath to return to the forest. This was the fifth day of our fast; so much the worse for us; it was time to put an end to it, so we made our way to an abandoned farm. We sheltered there for two hours, scanning the surrounding country for signs of life. Everything seemed dead.

We could see no peasant, no civilian, not even an animal, and this waiting was one torment the more, but it was to be the last. Not till ten o'clock, over there, very far off, did I catch sight of the thin black caterpillar of a column of soldiers coming our way during my turn of sentry-go. My heart beat violently, but I refrained from giving the news to my comrades from the fear of raising false hopes. My eyes burnt like flame and my teeth chattered. If these were Germans the game was up. If they were French, oh! then!

I looked, I looked with my eyes pressing out of my head. At times, as I strained my eyes, everything grew misty and I could see nothing; then, a second later, I again found this growing caterpillar and I began to distinguish details. There were squadrons of cavalry, but I could not yet make out the colour; and my body, from being icy cold, turned to burning hot. At times I forced myself not to look. I looked again, counted twenty, and then devoured space with my eyes.

A patrol had been detached, and approached rapidly at the trot; this time I recognised French Hussars. Then all strength of will, and all my effort to remain calm disappeared, I turned my reeling head towards my comrades and I fell on the grass crying, crying like a madman, in words without sequence. The fatigue of these five days without food or drink, almost without sleep, and the living in a perpetual nightmare, brought on a nervous crisis, and my whole body was racked with spasms. My comrades, not having as yet understood, looked at me with astonishment. With a gesture I pointed out the approaching column, the pale blue of which contrasted brightly with the gold of the leaves.

All of them, as soon as they had seen it, were overcome as I had been, each in his own way. Some burst into brusque convulsive sobs, others danced, waving their arms like madmen or rather like poor wretches who have passed days of suffering and agony on a raft in midocean, and who suddenly see a ship approaching to their rescue.

# CHAPTER 4

# The Epic of a Young Girl

10TH SEPTEMBER TO 20TH OCTOBER, 1914

The battle finished on the tenth, and then the pursuit of the conquered army commenced and kept the whole world in suspense, with eyes fixed on this headlong flight towards the north, which lasted till the end of the month, and which was to be the prelude of the great battles of the Yser.

The region round Verberie was definitely cleared of Germans and was become once more French. The little town for some days presented an extraordinary spectacle.

We entered the town after having received the formal assurance of the 5th Chasseurs, who went farther on, that all the country was in our hands. Some divisional cyclists were seated at the roadside. We asked them for news of the 22nd, and their reply wrung our hearts. They knew nothing definite, but they had met a country cart full of our wounded comrades, who had told them that the regiment had been cut up.

No one could tell us where the divisional area was to be found. The division itself appeared to have been dismembered, lost and in part destroyed. We thought that we were the only survivors of a disaster, and, once the horses were in shelter in an empty abandoned farm stuffing themselves with hay, we wandered sadly through the streets destroyed by bombardment and by fire in search of such civilians as might have remained behind during the invasion.

A little outside the town we at last found a farm where two of the inhabitants had stayed on. The contrast between them was touching. One was a paralysed old man unable to leave his fields, the other was a young girl of fifteen, a frail little peasant, and rather ugly. Her strange green eyes contrasted with an admirable head of auburn hair, and she had heroically insisted on looking after her infirm grandfather, though all the rest of the family had emigrated towards the west. She had remained faithful to her duty in spite of the bombardment, the battle at their very door and the ill-treatment of the Bavarian soldiers who were billeted in the farm. Distressed, yet joyous, she prepared a hasty meal and busied herself in quest of food, for it was anything but easy to satiate eleven men dying of hunger when the Germans, who lay hands on everything, had only just left.

She wrung the neck of an emaciated fowl which had escaped massacre, and, by adding thereto some potatoes from the garden, she served us a breakfast, washed down with white wine, which made us stammer with joy, like children. One needs to have fasted for five days to have felt the cutting pains of hunger and of thirst in all their horror, to appreciate the happiness that one can experience in eating the wing of a scraggy fowl and in drinking a glass of execrable wine tasting like vinegar. She bustled about, and her pitying and motherly gestures touched our hearts. While we ate, she told us the most astonishing story that ever was, a story acted, illustrated by gestures, which made the scenes live with remarkable vividness.

She told us how, faithful to her oath, she was alone when the Bavarians came knocking at her door, how she lived three days with them, a butt for their innumerable coarsenesses, sometimes brutally treated when the soldiers were sober, sometimes pursued by their gross assiduities when they were drunk; how one night she had to fly half naked through the rain, slipping out through the vent-hole of the cellar, to escape being violated by a group of madmen, not daring to go to bed again, sleeping fully dressed behind a small copse; how at last French *chasseurs* had put the Bavarians to flight and had in their turn installed themselves in the farm, and how among them she felt herself protected and respected.

She attached herself to her new companions, whom she

looked after like a mother for three days. Then they went away, promising to return, and she was left alone.

But the next day at dawn, uneasy at the row that came from the town, she decided to go in search of news. She put on a shawl and slipped through the brushwood and thickets as far as the first houses. She was afraid of being seen, and made herself as small as possible, keeping close to the walls, crossing gardens and ruined houses. The terrible noise increased, and she went towards it. She wanted to see what was going on, and a fine virile courage sustained her. The shells fell near her; no matter, she had only a few more steps to go to turn the corner of a street. She arrived on the *place* as the battle was finishing.

Her fifteen *chasseurs* were there, fifteen corpses at the foot of the barricade. One of them, who still lived, raised himself on seeing her, and held out his arms towards her. Then, forgetting all danger, in a magnificent outburst of feminine pity, she braved the rain of fire and dashed to the centre of the place. She knelt by the young fellow, enveloped him in her shawl to warm him and rocked him in her arms till he closed his young eyes for ever, thankful for this feminine presence which had made his last sufferings less bitter.

While she remained kneeling on the pavement wet with blood, a last big calibre shell knocked over, almost at her feet, a big corner house, which in its fall buried the German and French corpses in one horrible heap. She fell in a faint on the stones, knocked over by the windage of the shell, which had so nearly done for her.

During the latter part of her discourse she straightened her thin figure to the full, her strange eyes sparkled, and she appeared to be possessed by some strong and mysterious spirit which made us tremble. She became big in her rustic simplicity—big, as the incarnation of grief and of pity, and the peasant in her gave place to a living image of the war—an image singularly moving and singularly beautiful.

★★★★★★

From the next day Verberie became in some degree the rallying point for all soldiers who had lost touch with their units. Elements of all sorts of regiments, of all arms, of all races even, arrived on foot, on horseback, on bicycles, in country carts. There were dragoons, *cuirassiers*, *chasseurs*, artillerymen, Algerian Light Infantry and English. *Bernous*, khaki uniform, blue capes, rubbed shoulders with dolmans, black tunics and red trousers.

In this extraordinary crowd there were men from Morocco mounted on Arab horses and wearing turbans; there were *"Joyeux"* who wore the *tarboosh*, and ruddy English faces surmounted by flat caps. All the uniforms were covered with dirt and slashed and torn. Many of the men had bare feet, and some carried arms and some were without. It was the hazard of the colossal Battle of the Marne, where several millions of men had been at grips, which had thrown them on this point. All were animated by the same desire for information, and particularly of the whereabouts of their respective regiments.

From every direction flowed in convoys, waggons, artillery ammunition waggons, stragglers from every division and from every army corps. The mix-up and the confusion were indescribable. One heard shouting, swearing, neighing of horses, the horns of motorcars, and the rumble of heavy waggons, which shook the houses.

Faces drawn with fatigue were black with dust and mud and framed in stubbly beards. Everyone was gesticulating, everyone was shouting and a bright autumn sun, following upon the storm, threw into prominence amongst the medley of clothing the luminous splashes of gaudy colours and imparted an Oriental effect to the crowd.

★★★★★★

Having eaten, washed and rested, I walked the streets, drinking the morning air and taking deep breaths of the *joie de vivre,* of the strength and vitality mingled with the air. I looked on every side to see whether I could not find some acquaintance in the crowd, some stray trooper from my regiment.

So it was that the hazard of my walk brought me to a scene which moved me to tears and which rests graven so deeply on my memory that I can see its smallest detail with my eyes shut. The Gothic porch of the church, with its fine sculptures of the best period, was open, making in the brightness of the morning a pit of shade, at the foot of which some candles shone like stars. On the threshold of the porch, gaily lighted by the morning sun, a priest, whose fine virile face I can still recall, held in his hand the enamel pyx, and his surplice of lace of a dazzling whiteness contrasted with the muddy boots and spurs. One could guess that after having traversed some field of battle, consoling the wounded and the dying, he had dismounted to officiate in the open air under the morning sun.

Before him, on a humble country cart and lying on a bed of straw, were stretched the rigid bodies, fixed in death, of two *chasseurs* who had fallen nobly while defending the bridge over the river. All around, kneeling in the mud of the porch, a semi-circle of bareheaded soldiers, overcome by gratitude and humility, were assembled to accomplish a last duty and pay their last respects to the two comrades who were lying before them and who were sleeping their last sleep in their bloodstained uniforms, and assisted at the supreme office. The priest finished the *De profundis*, and in a clear voice pronounced the sacred words *"Revertitur in terrain suam unde erat et spiritus redit ad Deum qui dedit illum."* The officiant gave the holy-water sprinkler to the priest, who sprinkled the bodies and murmured *"Requiescat in pace,"* "Amen," responded the kneeling crowd, and a great wave of religious feeling passed over the kneeling men, the greater part of whom gave way to overmastering emotion.

I can still see a big devil of an artilleryman, with his head between his hands, shaken by convulsive sobs. Having given the absolution, the priest raised the host sparkling in the sunlight for the last time and pronounced the sacramental words. I moved off, deeply affected by the grandeur of the scene.

★★★★★★

By the 12th a good number of 22nd Dragoons and some officers of the regiment had rejoined at Verberie. We formed from this debris an almost complete squadron under the command of Captain de Salverte, who had succeeded in getting through the lines by skirting the forest.

I again found my officer, M. Chatelin, whom I had last seen

FRENCH CUIRASSIERS EARLY IN THE WAR

in the little clearing near Gilocourt, surrounded by lurking enemies, and whom I had hardly dared hope to see again alive; also M. de Thézy, my comrade Clère and others.

We were all sorry to hear that Lieutenant Roy had fallen on the field of battle with several others, and that Major Jouillié had been taken prisoner. As for Captain de Tarragon, it was stated that he might have escaped on foot with his orderly and that he might be somewhere in the neighbourhood with a contingent of escaped men, but any precise information was wanting.

The night before I had slept in the drawing-room of the *château* belonging to M. de Maindreville, the mayor. Its appearance merits some brief description, so that those who are still in doubt as to the savagery of the Germans may learn to what degree of bestiality and ignominy, they are capable of attaining.

This fine drawing-room was a veritable dung heap. The curtains were torn, the small billiard-table lay upside down in the middle of the room, a litter of rotting food covered the floor, the furniture was in matchwood, the chairs were broken, the easy-chairs had had their stuffing torn out of them and the glass of the cabinets was smashed. One could see that all small objects had been carried off and all others methodically broken.

On the first floor the sight was heart-breaking. Fine linen, trimmed with lace, was soiled with excrement; excrement was everywhere, in the bath, on the sheets, on the floor. They had vomited on the beds and urinated against the walls; broken bottles had shed seas of red wine on the costly carpets. An unnameable liquid was running down the staircase, obscene designs were traced in charcoal on the wall-papers and filthy inscriptions ornamented the walls.

I have told enough to give an idea of the degrading traces left by a contemptible enemy. I have exaggerated nothing; if anything, I have understated the truth.

And this is the people that wants to be the arbiter of culture and of civilisation! May it stand for ever shamed and reduced to its true level, which is below that of the brute beast.

★★★★★★

On the morning of the 12th, under the command of Captain

de Salverte we crossed the Oise by a bridge of boats, the stone bridge having been destroyed by dynamite some days before. We went north to billet at Estrée-Saint-Denis, which was to be the definite rallying point of the 22nd Dragoons. We were followed by several country carts, full of dismounted troopers, saddles, lances, cloaks and odds and ends of equipment.

Acting on very vague information, I set out on the 13th to look for Captain de Tarragon. I was mounted on a prehistoric motor bicycle, requisitioned from the village barber. I scoured the country seeking information from everyone I met. I received the most contradictory reports, made a thousand useless detours and was exasperated when overtaken by night without having found any trace of him.

I followed the road leading to Baron and to Nanteuil-le-Haudoin, along which but a few days before the corps of Landwehr, asked for by von Kluck, had marched with the object of enveloping our army, and along which it had just been precipitately hustled back. The sky was overcast and the day threatening. At each step dead horses with swelled bellies threatened heaven with their stiff legs. A score of soldiers were lying in convulsed attitudes, their eyes wide open, with grimacing mouths twisted into a terrifying smile, and with hands clasping their rifles. Involuntarily I trembled at finding myself alone at nightfall in this deserted country, where no living being was to be seen, where not a sound was to be heard except the cawing of thousands of crows and the purr of my motor, which panted on the hills like an asthmatic old man, causing me the liveliest anxiety.

Fifteen hundred metres from Baron, after a last gasp, my machine stopped for ever, and, as I was ignorant of its mechanics, I was compelled to leave it where it was and continue my journey on foot through the darkness.

The proprietor of the *château* of Baron put me up for the night. As at Verberie, everything had been burnt, soiled and destroyed. Nothing remained of the elegant furniture beyond a heap of shapeless objects. Next morning with the aid of a captain on the staff who requisitioned a trap for me, I got back to Verberie and found Captain de Tarragon there. He had slept at the farm of La Bonne Aventure, quite near to where I lay.

When he saw me, after the mortal anxieties through which he had lived, believing his squadron lost and cut up, he was overcome by such a feeling of gratitude and joy that I saw tears rise to his eyes while he shook me vigorously by the hand. He had already sent forward my name for mention in the order for the day with reference to the affair at Gilocourt and the death of poor Dangel. I was recommended for the military medal, and my heart swelled with pride and joy, while I was carried back to Estrée-Saint-Denis, stretched out in a country cart with a score of dismounted comrades.

A few days afterwards I was promoted corporal and proudly sported the red flannel chevrons bought at a country grocer's shop.

★★★★★★

Once the half-regiment was reconstituted after a fashion, though many were missing (a detachment of fifty men without horses having returned to the depot), we were attached to the 3rd Cavalry Division, which happened to be in our neighbourhood, ours having left the area for some unknown destination. Until the1st of October our lot was bound up with that of the 4th Cuirassiers, who marched with us.

On the 23rd of September, as supports for the artillery, we were present at violent infantry actions between Nesle and Billancourt. The 4th Corps attacked, and the furious struggle extended over the whole country. My troop was detached as flank guard and, in the thick morning fog, we knocked up against a handful of German cavalry, whom, in the distance, we had taken for our own men.

We charged them at a gallop, and we noticed that they were tiring and that we were gaining on them. One of them drew his sabre and cut his horse's flanks with it, whilst a non-commissioned officer turned and fired his revolver without hitting us; but, thanks to the fog, they got away. We did not tempt providence by following them too far for fear of bringing up in their lines.

At night we were sent to reconnoitre some fires which were

reddening the horizon and which, from a distance, seemed vast conflagrations. We came upon a bivouac of Algerian troops, who were squatting on their heels, warming themselves, singing strange African melodies and giving to this corner of French soil an appearance of Algeria.

On hearing the sound of our horses, they sprang to arms with guttural cries, but when they had recognised that we were French they insisted on embracing our officer and danced round us like children.

We billeted at Parvillers in a half-destroyed farm, and there at daybreak a sight that suggested an hallucination met our eyes. Some ten German soldiers were there in the courtyard dead, mowed down by the "75," but in such natural attitudes that but for their waxen colour one could have believed them alive. One was standing holding on to a bush, his hand grasping the branches. His face bespoke his terror, his mute mouth seemed as if in the act of yelling and his eyes were dilated with fear. A fragment of shell had pierced his chest. Another was on his knees, propped against a wall, under cover of which he had sought shelter from the murderous fire.

I approached to see where his wound was and it took me a moment to discover it, so intact was the corpse. I saw at last that he had had the whole of the inside of his cranium carried away and hollowed out, as if by some surgical instrument. His tongue and his eyes were kept in place by a filament of flesh, and his spiked helmet had rolled off by his side. An officer was seated on some hay, with his legs apart and his head thrown back, looking at the farm.

All these eyes fixed us with a terrifying immobility, with a look of such acute terror that our men turned away, as if afraid of sharing it; and not one of them dared to touch the magnificent new equipment of the Germans, which would have tempted them in any other circumstances. There were aluminium water-bottles and mess tins, helmet plates of shining copper and sculptured regimental badges dear to the hearts of soldiers, and which they have the habit of collecting as trophies.

The dawn of the 25th broke without a cloud over the village

FRENCH DRAGOONS AND GERMAN UHLANS SKIRMISH

of Folies. A heat haze hid the early morning sun. The enemy were quite near, and the sentries on the barricades gave the alarm. The *cuirassiers* and dragoons, leaving their horses under cover, had been on watch in the surrounding country since the morning to protect the village and the batteries of "75's," which were firing from a little way back.

A non-commissioned officer and I had remained mounted. M. de Thézy sent us to investigate some horsemen whose shadows had loomed through the mist and whom we had seen dismount in an apple orchard near the village of Chocques. We set off at a quiet trot, convinced that we had to deal with some French hussars whom I had seen go that way an hour before. We crossed a field of beetroot and made straight towards them. They seemed anchored to the spot, and when we were within one hundred metres, and they showed no signs of moving, our confidence increased. The fog seemed to grow thicker and our horses, now at the walk, scented no danger.

We were within fifty metres of them when a voice spoke out and the word "carbine" reached us distinctly, carried by a light breeze. The non-commissioned officer turned to me, his suspicions completely stilled, and said, "We can go on, they are French, I heard the word carbine." At the same instant I saw the group come to the shoulder and a dozen jets of fire tore the mist with short red flashes. A hail of bullets fell all around us, and we had only just time enough to put between them and ourselves as much fog as would conceal us, for before turning tail we had seen the confused grey mass of a column coming out of the village. We had only to warn the artillery and then there would be some fun.

The lieutenant of artillery was two kilometres back perched on a ladder. Having listened to what we had to say, he turned towards his gun and cried through a megaphone, "2600, corrector 18." We were already far off, returning at the gallop to try to see the effect, and it was a fine sight.

Leaving the horses in a farm, we slipped from tree to tree. There was the column, still advancing. A first shell, ten metres in front of it, stopped it short; immediately a second fell on the left, wounding some men, and a horse reared and upset its rider. A third shell struck mercilessly into the centre of the column and caused an explosion which sent flying, right and left, dark shapes which we guessed to be fragments of bodies. It rained shell, which struck the road with mathematical precision, sowing death and panic. In the twinkling of an eye the road was swept clean. The survivors bolted in every direction like madmen, and the agonising groans of a dying horse echoed through the whole countryside.

★★★★★★

On the 1st of October we rejoined our division and the first half-regiment at Tilloy-les-Mofflaines. Up to the 20th we passed through a period of great privation and fatigue owing to the early frosts. We were unable to sleep for as many as five days on end, and when at night we had a few hours in which to rest, we passed them lying on the pavement of the street, propped up against some heap of coal or of stones, holding our horses' reins, each huddled up against his neighbour to try and keep warm.

Here are extracts from my diary, starting from 8th October:

*8th October,*—All night we guarded the bridge at Estaires, after having constructed a formidable barricade. Damp and chilly night, which I got through lying on the pavement before the bridge; drank a half-litre of spirits in little sips to sustain me. This is the most trying night we have passed, but the spirits of all are wonderful.

*9th October,*—*Twenty minutes to four, two kilometres from Estaires, scouting amongst beetroot fields.*—Has the supreme moment come? A little while ago I firmly believed that it had; now I am out of my reckoning, so incomprehensible and widespread is the struggle which surrounds us.

We have evacuated Estaires and the bridge over the Lys, which we were guarding, to rejoin our horses on foot. After some minutes on the road the first shells burst. My troop received orders to fight dismounted, and here we are, lying down as skirmishers amongst the beetroot, in the midst of a heavy artillery and musketry fire. I am on the extreme right, and a moment ago two shrapnel shells came over and burst six or eight metres above my head, peppering the ground with bullets. Never, I imagine, have I come so near to being hit.

For the moment it is impossible to understand what is going on; the whole of the cavalry which was on in front of us—*chasseurs*, dragoons and all the cyclists—have fallen back, passing along the road on our flank. We, however, have had no order to retire. The peasants with their wives and children are running about the country like mad people. It is a sorry sight. A moment ago, I saw an old man and a little girl fall in their hurry to escape from their farm, which a shell had just knocked to pieces. They are like herds of animals maddened by a storm.

At dusk the Germans are 500 metres off. We have orders to take up our post in the cemetery of Estaires. I have hurt my foot and each step in the ploughed land is a torture. I have noted a way which will lead me to the bridge on the other side of the town.

I brought up my patrol at the double. When I got back, I saw the troop retiring.

We passed through the town, which had a sinister look by night, reddened by the flames from many fires. The whole population is in flight, leaving houses open to the streets, and crowding up the roads. All the window-panes are broken by the bombardment; somewhere, in the middle of the town, a building is burning and the flames mount to the sky. There are barricades in every street. We have reached the horses, which are two kilometres from the town, and we grope for them in the dark. Mine is slightly wounded in the foreleg. Long retreat during the night (the second during which we have not slept—a storm wets us to the skin).

Arrived at Chocques at five in the morning. We get to bed at 6.30 and we are off again at 8 o'clock. I ask myself for how many days men and horses can hold out.

*10th October,*—In the afternoon we again covered the twenty kilometres which separated us from Estaires. Hardly had we settled down to guard the same bridge as yesterday when we were sent to La Gorgue. On the way stopped in the village, as shells commenced to fall. The 1st troop took refuge in a grocer's, where we were parked like sheep. A large calibre shell burst just opposite with a terrible row. I thought that the house was going to fall in. Lieutenant Niel, who had stayed outside, was knocked over into the ditch and wounded. We are falling back with the horses to La Gorgue, and we are passing a third night, without sleep, on the road, Magrin and I on a heap of coal. Horses and men have had nothing to eat, the latter are benumbed, exhausted, but gay as ever.

*11th October,*—We get to a neighbouring farm at Estrem to feed the horses. They have scarcely touched their hay and oats before an order comes telling us to rejoin at the very place from which we have come. The Germans are trying to take the village from the east, thanks to the bridge which they captured the day before yesterday, but we have been reinforced by cyclists, and the 4th Division is coming up. We are holding on; the position is good. The belfry of the town hall has just fallen. We are going back to Estrem.

Three hours passed in a trench without great-coats. Magrin and I are so cold that we huddle up one against the other and share a woollen handkerchief to cover our faces. We put up at Calonne-sur-la-Lys. And so, it goes on up to the 17th, the date on which we re-enter Belgium, passing by Bailleul, Outersteene and Locre. It is not again a triumphal entry on a fine August morning, it is a march past ruins and over rubbish heaps.

At Outersteene, however, we were received with touching manifestations of confidence and enthusiasm; an old tottering and broken-down teacher had drawn up before the school a score of young lads of seven to ten years old, who watched us passing and sang the *Marseillaise* with all their lungs, while the old man beat the time.

The village had been evacuated only three days ago, and it was from the thresholds of its houses, partly fallen in and still smoking, that this song rose, a sincere and spontaneous outburst.

# CHAPTER 5

# The Two Glorious Days of Staden

On October 19th, at midday, we rode into Hougled. The captain got us together and warned us that we were being sent on in front to delay the march of the enemy till our infantry had had time to come up. The enemy's march had to be delayed *at all costs*. He did not conceal from us that two, or perhaps three, divisions had been marked down in front of us, that the task would be a stiff one and that it was a question of "sticking it out" to the last drop of our blood.

We then received orders to prepare for a dismounted action, and, leaving our horses in a street, we set off across the ploughed fields, laden with ammunition. I carried a big cartridge case, which I usually left in my wallets on account of its weight.

Some round clouds, of a snowy whiteness, which made them stand out against the crude and washy blue of the background, scudded across the sky, carried by a stiff breeze. All Nature was *en fête*, and the fresh strong wind was intoxicating.

Towards four o'clock the enemy showed himself in sections and in companies, well aligned on the plain beneath us. There was no attempt at concealment, as, doubtless, the village was thought to be unoccupied.

Under cover of some thin brushwood we opened fire on these regular formations, to show that we were there and not in the least impressed by these demonstrations of company and field training. It was just like being on manoeuvres, and these awkward soldiers seemed rather ridiculous, gravely doing the goose-step, when so soon it would be a question of killing or being killed.

We must have got their range, for we noted through field-glasses a slight confusion in the enemy's ranks, and, instantaneously, the advancing infantry disappeared. They were still there, however, for their bullets, slipping over the ridge where we offered a good target, pitted the turf all round us, happily without wounding anyone. The Germans have a remarkable faculty of making themselves scarce in the twinkling of an eye as soon as they have been seen by an enemy, like those insects which, at the least noise, blend with the grass on which they are perched.

Our naval guns, ranged by the side of the road, fired over the plain. An observing officer, standing on his horse's back, judged the effects of the fire. We saw the shells burst in beautiful plumes of dark or light smoke. The enemy's fusillade ceased, much to our satisfaction.

But the German artillery began to reply, and we were soon subjected to such a fire that we had to retreat towards the village, being uneasy about our horses, which happened to be in the line of fire. In going along the main street, we kept close to the walls to avoid the shell splinters. Shells of all calibres fell without ceasing, making holes in the thin slate roofs and breaking the windows. I saw one pierce a wall some paces in front of me and burst inside a house, whose stories collapsed, one on the top of the other. It was just like an earthquake, the whole street was shaken by it.

We made for our horses at the double and found them plunging under this storm of fire, and we galloped off behind the village to get them into safety. Without losing a second we distributed extra cartridges in large numbers and returned to take our place between the farms in the grass fields shut in by hedges and barriers. We worked at fortifying our positions till evening. Everyone made "his trench." (That word had then another signification; at that time the word trench represented for us the least scooped-out hole, the least obstacle placed between the enemy and us.)

We protected ourselves with sand-bags, faggots, agricultural implements, etc. We were hardly installed before we received an order to leave this place and to occupy a road on the right, running between two meadows. We made a barricade at the end of it, somehow or other, with whatever came to hand.

The infantry, expected at four o'clock, were late, and it became questionable whether it would be materially possible to hold out much longer, if the Germans attacked, taking into consideration the disproportion between our forces and those of the enemy.

Night had hardly come when an infernal fusillade broke out, and it lasted till daylight without the least slackening. It was exactly like an uninterrupted salvo fire, with the addition of the sharp, regular dry crackle of machine-guns. Thousands of projectiles struck our fragile barricade or passed, whistling, over our heads. We fired straight in front of us into the dark night, without knowing what we aimed at, except that our fire was directed towards the place whence this murderous storm of shot and shell came.

Constantly the same question ran from man to man: "Have the infantry come up?" for we knew that our lives depended on their arrival. Our orders were: "You will prevent the Germans passing till you have been relieved."

We had only a handful of troopers, two hundred perhaps, to check the onslaught of a formidable mass of infantry. Unless our infantry came to our aid we would be cut up to a man; but the enemy should have to pass over our bodies.

Overcome with fatigue, and in spite of the thunder all round us, I fell asleep, suddenly, heavily, dreamlessly, in a little ditch which ran by the roadside. I don't know when I awoke. The noise of the combat was dominated by a clamour still louder and more penetrating: a part of the village of Staden was on fire. A horde of Germans dashed into it, yelling "Hourraa!" A diabolical clamour rose to heaven, and yells and cries of bestial joy mounted with the thick smoke of the fires.

We learnt afterwards that they had charged empty barricades, a party of our men having evacuated the town an hour previously. A corporal of the 1st squadron, posted a little more to the left, told me he had seen them 200 yards off defiling in quick step "silhouetted like devils" against the glare of the fire.

Still no infantry.

A torpor seized me and I fell back into the ditch, overcome by sleep, and slept again till almost daylight. From that moment events moved with great rapidity. It must have been seven o'clock when the infantry at last arrived, fifteen hours late. We heard hurried footsteps. I turned and saw troops falling back in hot haste, being irresistibly outflanked by the enemy. They seemed to be pursued by assailants who were on their heels. I heard voices exclaiming, "It is pitiable to see fellows so up against it." I said nothing, but, in my inner consciousness, I clearly understood that the supreme moment was come for many of us.

For a moment I feared that we had been forgotten in the general movement. Soon afterwards Captain de Tarragon appeared at the cross-roads. I can see him still; he looked immensely big in his blue cloak. Without speaking, he signalled to us that we could retire. It was time indeed, for the enemy outflanked us on all sides. The troop doubled towards him and ran on. Magrin and I remained alongside him. Never so much as then have I felt the irresistible force of Destiny. It was written that I was to remain with him until the end.

We three reached a farm on the crest of the ridge; 400 metres off a German company was advancing. The captain seized a carbine from the hands of a late-comer who fled past us and turned round to open fire. Faithful to my oath, and knowing that our lives hung on a thread, I fired off the contents of my magazine alongside of him. I aimed as best I could, though my greatcoat interfered, and I shot into the brown. A second later the German reply crumbled the wall of the farm, passing between the captain and me, two fingers' breadth over our heads.

I implored de Tarragon not to expose himself any longer. What was the use of this heroic folly of standing up alone against an advancing battalion of the enemy? Doubtless our regiment was already a long way off, but we might, perhaps, be able to rejoin it by crawling along the deep ditch which ran by the roadside.

STADEN - L'ÉGLISE
THE CHURCH

Hate of the enemy seemed, however, to rage in his heart, and he replied, "It is too bad to have to abandon such a target!" At last, his cartridges being exhausted, he decided to retire, without running, and seeming to defy the entire world with his tall well set-up figure of a handsome French soldier. Instead of taking to the ditch which ran by the roadside, he crossed the field of fire. I followed him, without understanding, and Magrin did likewise.

A moment afterwards our number was increased to four by the arrival of an officer of hussars or of *chasseurs*, who came running up. All my life I shall remember this last. He was young, elegant and good-looking, and so trim and neat with his sky-blue cap jauntily set at an angle. When two metres off he opened his mouth as if to speak, but before having emitted a sound he fell dead, hit by a bullet under the ear.

The captain, who was at my side, stepped forward to put himself, at last, under shelter. Hardly had he taken a step before a bullet hit him, and I uttered a cry of rage on seeing him fall in a heap. Feigning to be wounded or dead, to deceive the enemy and cause the cessation of his fire, I fell also, and both of us rolled into the deep ditch.

There was not a minute to lose. "Magrin, quick, quick, no good troubling about the lieutenant of *chasseurs*, he's dead; but perhaps the captain is still alive, we must get him away." Magrin, who had tumbled down after me, believing me hit, raised the captain's head and I took his feet. A hail of bullets passed like a squall above our heads. We stayed so a good five minutes, exhausting ourselves in useless efforts to carry off this inert body. On account of its weight it was impossible even to move it in the squatting and unhandy position in which we found ourselves.

He did not regain consciousness for an instant; once his eyes opened, then the eyelids quivered and his head fell back heavily. He was dead, and we could not think of getting him away. The fire was furious. Magrin and I, who had remained behind till the last, now tried to gain the farm behind which our regiment was massed. We made three metres under cover of the ditch, and then we covered a hundred metres at the run, under such a rain of bullets, aimed at us, that I attribute our escape to a miracle. My greatcoat and cape were riddled. As I turned the corner of the house, that corner even was torn off and the broken bricks fell on me. I passed by some bicycles abandoned against a wall, and, after I had gone by, I heard the sharp crack of broken spokes, which the bullets had cut.

Once I had passed the corner, I found shelter for an instant. I came across Captain Besnier who was wounded, and helped to carry him. The road was strewn with the bodies of dragoons, *chasseurs* and cyclists. Behind the house were a brick-field and a clay-pit, whose slippery crest had to be crossed. I saw some un-lucky fellows get half over, within two paces of safety, and then roll to the bottom, hit by the pitiless machine-guns.

The firing redoubled. Major Chapin, who had arrived at the front only three days before, fell hit through the head, and many others fell whom I did not know.

The command of our party devolved on Lieutenant Mi-elle, and, following an order from the dying Major Chapin, we took the direction of the railway bridge on the right. Lieuten-ant Desonney was wounded and lay out a hundred metres off. I heard the colonel cry in a loud voice with an accent of despair which is untranslatable, "Won't someone bring in Desonney?" and one after the other five dragoons unhesitatingly left their shelter and threw themselves into the furnace of fire, each of them as he fell, within a few yards, and to be immediately re-placed by another. The whole regiment would have gone if the colonel had not put a stop to such heroic obedience.

But what was going on? Amidst the noise of battle the clear notes of a bugle mounted to heaven; both sides hesitated. They were the well-known notes sounding the charge. We turned, and a sight of unspeakable grandeur met our eyes.

The dismounted 1st squadron, lance in hand, charged into the whirlwind of fire, to allow of the rest of the regiment fall-ing back. The obsessing refrain made one's temples throb. We were hypnotised, and the colonel, standing up, unconscious of the bullets which grazed him, folded his arms and watched his admirable soldiers who, moved by almost superhuman brotherly devotion, braved the fire and retarded for a moment the enemy's march so as to permit their comrades to escape. The colonel watched, and great tears of pride and of anxiety ran down his tanned cheeks. When, once in one's life, one has had the privilege of seeing such a deed, it lives with one for ever.

We now crawled across the railway. The machine-guns mowed the fields of beetroot as if they had been shaved off with a razor. Seven of us took this way and we all got through, I don't know how, without being touched. Then we slipped between the infantry sections which were advancing in skirmishing order on all sides. Some minutes later we were behind a ridge under cover and in safety. We reached a little shanty where we sheltered for a long time, and from the loft of which we could still fire on the enemy.

Towards 9 o'clock the musketry fire gradually diminished. We left the farm only when the artillery duel began. The shells came a bit too close, and there was the risk of the house falling in on us.

We went in search of the horses two kilometres off, and retirement was decided on because of the need for food and rest. When I caught up the column at the trot, I counted 47 led horses, which means that 47 men had fallen. Desonney's troop had an officer and 14 men missing out of 28. We had lost a major, two captains, two lieutenants and many comrades, but we had made it possible for two army corps to come up.

A mere handful of men had put up a fight against three divisions. A fine page in the history of the regiment!

My greatcoat was handed round the squadron. A bullet had pierced the cloth four times under the heart, another twice through the arm, three others over the ribs.

★★★★★★

Eight days afterwards, at Clarques, near Saint-Omer, where we were resting, promotions were made to replace the non-commissioned officers who had fallen gloriously that day. I was made sergeant-major.

## CHAPTER 6

# Ypres and the Neighbouring Sectors

A memorable ceremony in which with others of the regiment I took part, was on the occasion of the ceremony at Saint-Omer in honour of Field-Marshal Lord Roberts, who had died on the 15th November while on a visit to the allied armies.

At half-past six the regiment was formed up on the road and the twelve best specimens of manhood were picked out from each troop. We were soaked by rain on the way, but the sun came out when the ceremony began.

We were formed up in battle array before the town hall. All round the square, on the edge of the pavement, a single rank of Highlanders, carefully sized, stood like statues. We waited the coffin, which appeared at last from a side street, preceded by a troop of English cavalry who marched slowly—their black horses were admirable creatures. Then came a section of infantry, fine, big, taking fellows, who marched with their heads down and their eyes fixed on the ground; next came superb Indian troops, who wore turbans, amongst whom were great native princes; then a contingent of Canadians, just disembarked; lastly some Highland pipers playing a lament whose refrain was eternally alike. We had heard this shrill lament for a long time, now it became stronger and more penetrating the nearer the *cortège* approached, and gave a strange exotic note to this old-fashioned setting of a little French town.

When the coffin appeared the Highlanders, who formed the guard of honour executed a strange movement. They slowly described an arc of a circle with their rifles, their outstretched right arms forming an uninterrupted line all round the square, then each man finished the movement by crossing his arms on the butt-plate of his rifle, the muzzle of which was now resting on the ground.

With their heads bowed, these mourners resembled some old bas-relief. The coffin, enveloped in the Union Jack, was borne on a gun-carriage. It was all very simple and very moving.

To the wild notes of the Scottish bagpipes, now silent, the clear trumpets of our dragoons replied, and their sound was in itself like sparkling metal. They continued to sound until the remains of the field-marshal had been placed in the town hall.

After the ceremony, which we did not see, twenty-one guns thundered out, fired by batteries posted behind the square. An immense rainbow, as sharply defined as if drawn with a stroke of the brush, cut the sky with a perfect and uninterrupted semi-circle. Symbol of peace, it came to earth directly behind the batteries, and the flash of the guns showed up against its iridescent screen.

An English officer came to tell the colonel that the ceremony was over, and we returned to Clarques under a beating rain, which had begun to fall again.

Our next active work was at Nieuport. Motor buses brought us to Coxyde, where, amongst the slightly built villas of this watering-place, Belgian and French uniforms swarmed. Sand-dunes, on which the sand encroached on the scanty covering of grass, bordered the horizon on all sides.

Captain Vigoureux had sent me to lay out the camp with a corporal and one man. Clère, Hénon and I went on ahead at a sharp pace. From Coxyde to Ostdinkerque there was no trace of bombardment. On the road we met several lots of horses at exercise, some waggons, many soldiers and a few civilians. At Ostdinkerque a mill, two houses and a part of the church had been gutted yesterday. Some vehicles contained civilians, who were prudently clearing out.

From this place onwards (Nieuport-Ville was six kilometres off) the road became more and more deserted and the noise of the guns became louder. At first, we only heard the noise of our own batteries and the shell burst a long way off. Two kilometres from Nieuport I heard the whistle of the first German shell, a shrapnel which burst some hundreds of metres off. Several people on the road were peppered with the fragments of shell; the telegraph wires were broken and the rails of a tramway were torn up. The country was a desert, and the eye saw nothing but sand-dunes without end, and here our underground life began.

At the entrance to the town a prudent man on duty showed his profile at the door of a cellar. I asked him, "Where is Captain Mahot?" and he answered in an irritated voice: "Don't stand there in the middle of the road, don't you see that the shells are falling just where you are?" I had not noticed it, but I did not take long to find out. The man on duty led me five metres underground to Lieutenant Deporte.

"Sir, where is Captain Mahot? The town *commandant* of the 16th Dragoons? I see no one about."

"Everyone has gone to earth," he replied, placidly filling his pipe, "and I advise you to hurry up and do likewise, for it comes down like hail just about now."

It did indeed. I heard the most disquieting sounds, the bursting of big shells, the splash of bullets, which flattened themselves against the houses. Some streets were enfiladed, and thousands of shrapnel bullets flew back and forward between the German trenches and ours.

The lieutenant gave me a man to take me to the captain's cellar, which was at the other end of the town. He and I (I had left the others in a cellar) skirted the walls, and at every step what a sight! All that remained of the church resembled a sort of historic ruin—some pillars, some arches, very fine ones, and some sculptures lying on the ground. Everywhere the craters of the big shells had the dimensions of dried-up ponds. In the principal *place* there were two such, in which one could have put two houses.

Speaking of houses, some had been destroyed with an art and a refinement which made them look like builder's models. One was standing, of which the only thing wanting was the outside wall facing the street, and one could see the section of the gaping interior. The pictures were hanging on the walls, and on the piano were photographs and knickknacks. The drawing-room, the dining-room and the bedroom were intact; but the flooring of the attics had given way and everything had fallen through to the floor below. Another house was almost comical in appearance, for, against a wall on the lowest storey, stood a fine bamboo rack, on which two statuettes of sham Saxeware smiled an eternal and idiotic smile and seemed to jeer at the bombardment.

Other houses, and these were the most numerous, were lamentable rubbish heaps, fallen in, blackened, broken up in every sense, blocking the streets and forming a hideous lamentable chaos. Even when no shell fell—and there were long moments of calm—the houses dropped to pieces of themselves. This one might lose the remainder of its tiles, which fell into the street with a din; the next one might drop, let us say, a stove, or a small billiard-table, from one floor to another.

I arrived at last at the end of my journey, having asked myself a thousand times whether I should not be pulverised on the way there. The worst bit was when I reached the last cross-roads. For the second time I asked an orderly whether this was the house—pardon, the cellar—of Captain Mahot, and for the second time I heard an irritated voice reply, "Don't stay there in the middle of the street"; but this time I lost the end of the phrase, being blinded and deafened.

The heavens seemed to fall on me. I heard, "Get under cover," and I felt my tympanum shattered. A house twenty metres from me, a large two-storeyed house, seemed to be transformed into a volcano. A shell had entered its middle, through the roof, and *the whole house collapsed into the street,* accompanied by a formidable fall of rafters, bricks and furniture.

"You see that," said the orderly in a severe tone; "get into the cellar." I felt just like a little boy.

Five marines had been buried under the ruins. A little later I saw their bodies on stretchers. What a lamentable death for a sailor or soldier!

Captain Mahot said to me, "The billeting area of the 22nd Dragoons? Very good, there it is," and he showed me the butt-end of street "the *shepstraat.*" I looked at it in astonishment, saying to myself, "That?" Messina after the earthquake would have offered more comfort. Nevertheless, I inspected the cellars and apportioned them amongst the troops, and, by myself this time, I returned through the town to my point of departure, to meet and conduct Captain Vigoureux, whom I found three hundred metres beyond the gates.

This made the fourth time that I had made this disquieting journey. I began to feel that I had had enough of it, the more so as I had walked twelve kilometres, and, not being accustomed to carrying a pack, my back hurt me. Clère was quite knocked up, and had looked at once so sad and so comic that I did not know whether to laugh at him or to pity him.

The regiment settled in more or less (rather less) in the sector reserved for it. The cellars were crowded. My orderly, who was a treasure of devotion and very inventive, arranged my kit, found me a candle and spread a mattress. I was kept on the run, everyone called me at once: "A man wanted for the guard-room, a liaison officer to see the captain, a man wanted for water fatigue, the quartermaster-sergeant wants to know how things are here, the 3rd troop have no billets and so on." . . . I tried to reply to everyone, and my head was like a whirlpool.

It was impossible to keep the men in, though there were strict orders that they were not to leave the cellars. They broke out in every direction, and, in spite of the shells, they amused themselves like children, entering the houses at the peril of their lives. One of them brought me a stuffed stork; another a cornet and a draught screen; my orderly came last with a woman's mantlet, trimmed with lace!

Towards six o'clock the rain of shells ceased.

After dinner not a sound was heard. The cold was cruel. I wrapped myself in my greatcoat and turned up the collar above my ears. I stuck my head well into my fatigue-cap and, to amuse myself, I started off on "reconnaissance," armed with an electric lamp. I visited twenty gutted houses, and this diversion was becoming monotonous when, from a particularly damaged court, I heard a somewhat uncertain hand playing the piano. The air

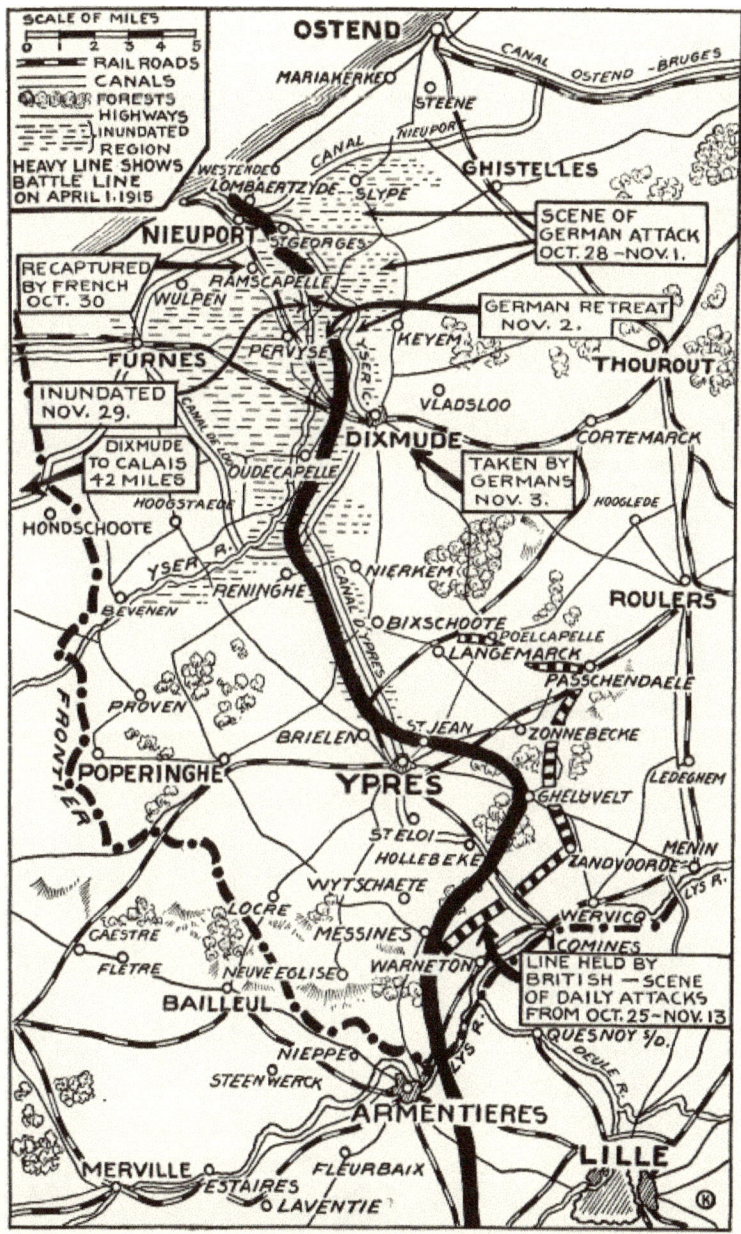

First Battle of Ypres

was one of those old waltzes which dragoons dote on and which suggest Viennese softness combined with the popular taste of the Boulevards. There was no light in the yawning house. One might have called it the house of Usher, at least I thought of that spontaneously, for there was something weird about those black holes from whence came this sad and popular jingle, though the eye was conscious of nothing but darkness.

My ideas wandered for a moment, but, noticing a ray of light at my feet, I found the key of the enigma: some *lascars* had brought the piano down to the cellar to be more at their ease. At the foot of some ten steps, or rather of a steep slope—I learnt afterwards that, in coming down stairs, the piano had done the work of a "105"—I had only to pull a canvas curtain aside slightly to see what was going on inside. It was an affecting scene.

Some ten men lay on mattresses listening to the musician, who was seated on a small cask, playing the same waltz over and over again, probably the only thing he knew, with his great clumsy fingers. There was something in the look of each of these men analogous to that of intoxication from opium, or to the fascination on his subject of a mesmerist. Above, the shells began to fall again; below, they had forgotten the war, because they listened to a tune they loved, and, music is all-powerful over simple hearts.

I remember this episode as one of the most picturesque souvenirs of the war. I stayed in that cellar playing to them for more than an hour. They were drunk with pleasure and with dreams of home. That night I could have led them to the assault, even to the cannon's mouth.

Next day, the 24th of January, *réveillé* was sounded at three o'clock.

At four o'clock we fell in. We were going into the second line trenches.

★★★★★★

Note:—Our "dug-out" was a little rectangular room five metres long by two metres wide, cut in the stiff soil, stayed up with planks, covered with beams and roofed with earth.

★★★★★★

On reading the remarkable and charming book which my colleague, Lieutenant Dupont, has published under the title *En Compagne*, I noticed in one chapter such a similarity of phrase that I thought of changing the beginning of this description, so as to avoid the appearance of a plagiarism. I decided, however, not to alter its first form, but to leave intact this page, which was written in the trenches on that very day 24th January, 1915, long before Lieutenant Dupont's book appeared

★★★★★★

It was dark as an oven. It was entered by an opening so narrow that my pack could not pass, and to get to this door, if one could call it a door, one had to perform prodigies from the roadside onwards to avoid being bogged up to the knees. There was a little straw on the floor, and the furniture consisted of a chair.

There we were going to take up our residence, my seven men and I—Dhuic, Laroche, Ponnery, Bobet, Thiérard, Emmanuel and that terrible-looking fellow Hurel, with his vulture's face and insane alcoholic eye. I can see him now at the bottom of the trench, his face emerging from a sheep-skin coat which made him look more than ever like a wild beast. "If the Bosches catch sight of you," an unindulgent comrade said to him, "they will certainly clear out in double-quick time."

We got here from Nieuport at four o'clock in the morning. The regiment was closed up and the men stumbled at each step over the debris of houses, which littered the road. Dead silence reigned, and the cold north wind of early morning made our eyes water. No shells or bullets were flying, but we heard from time to time the noise of tiles falling from some roof or the din of a falling skirt of wall. Star shell were being used, and each time they lit up the country they made us jumpy, for we presumed that they would be followed by a shell only too well placed.

Day dawned, and I came cautiously out of my hole to have a look at the country. The human imagination never, I imagine, has conceived, nor ever can picture, anything sadder or more desolate than what I saw. I found myself on the road leading from Nieuport to Saint-Georges at a point almost equally distant from both of these remains of towns. The banked-up road meandered over an immense muddy plain, flecked with pools of grey water, now frozen. Nieuport was on my right. From here I could not see a single house which was, I won't say intact, but only damaged by the bombardment. It was a heap of gutted buildings, crumbling walls and twisted and broken trees. On my left was Saint-Georges, in if anything worse state. Nothing remained but a pile of stones, and one would never have supposed that a village had once existed there.

By the side of my trench there was a freshly made grave, that is to say a square of mud surmounted by a white cross. The cap of a marine lay by its side. I picked it up; it was full of brains. The poor fellow must have been killed on this very spot, and yesterday probably, mown down perhaps by that same shell which had pierced two neighbouring trees with its murderous fragments.

As I re-entered my trench the sharp clatter of our batteries disturbed the air. They were placed quite near us, and well hidden, for I could see nothing of them. I supposed that this was the opening of the ball and that the enemy's reply would not be long in coming. Some of my men had come out. I made them get back again quickly, and treated Hurel to a kick from behind. The men become as quiet as sheep when there is danger about. One of them warmed me some coffee on a solid fuel spirit-lamp, and another let me make a pillow of his abdomen.

*25th January, 1915,*—We were relieved at 5 o'clock and returned safe and sound to Nieuport. I found the cellar transformed, thanks to Clère and Hénon; there was a light, a table covered with a cloth and some crockery. They had looted these things from the town, and I did not find fault with them for doing so, for these articles were safer where they were than in the ruins exposed at any moment to squalls of shell.

The bombardment had kept on increasing until past midday. It was dangerous to go outside. Every half-hour I made a round to make the men get back into their cellars. We made some tea, but the water came from the Yser, which was carrying down dead bodies, and the tea smelt of death. We could not drink it.

The ration cart arrived to an accompaniment of shells. We did not take long to unload it.

*26th January, 1915.*—At midday a French aeroplane flew over the dunes. It was bombarded at times, and it let fall some silver trails which sparkled in the sky like the scales of fish. (These were darts and position-indicating rockets.)

Tonight we buried a dragoon belonging to the 16th, who had been killed some days before in the course of a reconnaissance. The body was already at the cemetery, covered with earth, and we brought the coffin, carried by two soldier grave-diggers. It preceded, by some paces, the silent *cortège* formed by the Captain, M. Chatelin, the priest, two non-commissioned officers and myself. We crossed the canal bridge a little before midnight.

A sentry, petrified by cold, asked us for the countersign, which was given, and we went on our way, avoiding the white patches of moonlight which might have betrayed our presence.

The rusted gate of the cemetery creaked lamentably as we entered onto the holy ground that the shells had failed to respect. They had hollowed monstrous and gaping graves that yawned under our feet, laying bare, completely or partially, the skeletons and corpses. A stiff north wind was blowing, bending the slim shrubs and agitating the grass and the rotten crosses as in a dense macabre.

It was the devil of a night, and I admit that we all shivered, preferring the risks of a charge in full daylight to this sinister and furtive work. Every two or three minutes a star shell traced a lovely curve of diamonds in the sky, and, instinctively, we put our heads down in silence. Four men dug the grave. We uncovered the poor body, which had been covered with a thin layer of earth. It had been wrapped up in sacking, like the big quarters of beef that are unloaded from the supply carts when rations are given out.

It was the most lamentable thing I have ever seen.

Everything was hurried through in a few minutes. The coffin was too big. The captain put into it an envelope containing the name of the soldier who was going to rest there between the lines, and who would be crooned to sleep by the noise of shells.

The wind shook the surplice of the priest who recited the prayers, and I heard only a confused murmur of odd phrases, for the wind carried off the rest. We had to hurry, for the quiet moments were rare, and we returned through the dark deserted streets in impressive silence.

*Nieuport, 29th January, 1915.*—To form an exact idea of what this very peculiar war is like one must have lived the twenty-four hours that I have just passed through—a bitterly cold winter's day and night.

We set out to occupy the first line trenches at 4 o'clock. The night was clear and frosty, and the stars glittered like splinters of ice. A clear and cold moon lit up the immensity of the ravaged and desolated plain, making the ice glitter, silhouetting the traitorous and dangerous ruins, betraying our position by the glint from our bayonets, while the frost-bound ground conducted sound to a great distance.

As far as the post from which the second-line trenches were commanded the road was good and the distance easy; but from there onwards the carrying out of reliefs became hazardous. We marched in single file, holding our bayonets in our left hands to prevent them from knocking against our rifles, raising our feet and going on tiptoe, as in a sick-room. The road became atrociously bad, it being impossible to repair it owing to the nearness of the enemy. Nothing was wanting, ruts, holes, fencing wire, overturned fencing posts, etc. The squadron occupied some trenches on the right. These were arrow-shaped, and were the nearest trenches to the enemy.

Seventeen of us held the main trench, and in an adjacent one were two marines with a small pom-pom trench gun. These were called trenches; in reality they consisted of sloping beams laid against an embankment of stones and sand-bags. We had to crawl into them, and, once in, we were condemned to immobility. We could not even sit down without bending our heads. Little by little the cold took hold of us, beginning with our feet, and we felt as if we were transformed into blocks of ice.

The wind brought us a suggestive odour, which mingled with the smell of rotting litter on which we were lying. We felt inclined to vomit. Day came and brought the need for absolute immobility. It was impossible to risk oneself outside the trench, even flat on one's belly, until night-time. M. Chatelin and I shivered side by side, and inspected the horizon through field-glasses. On the left we saw some suspicious smoke, and the same distance off, on the right, we found the explanation of the stink we had smelt on our arrival.

A score of German corpses were there, caught between their barbed-wire entanglement and ours, and destined to rot there for an undetermined period. They were in all sorts of poses and horribly mutilated. Some bodies were without heads, some heads and arms were lying separated and all the bodies were in convulsive postures. A number of crows were disputing their bodies, as were some half-wild cats, which refused the meat we offered them—a pretty sight indeed; happily, there were no French bodies amongst them.

The artillery opened the ball about eight o'clock. We were almost in the middle, and well below the trajectory of the shells. We saw some shells strike their target—some farms, that fell to pieces—but many missed. That, however, was of no account.

From the direction of Lombaertzyde a sudden thunder re-sounded, and for the whole of the afternoon the earth was shaken by a bombardment which nothing could describe. To repre-sent it one must think of a furious sea, an express at full speed, lowing of cattle, catcalls, creakings; one must think of a mixture of all these sounds forming a sort of savage harmony. In the rays of the rising sun Lombaertzyde was crowned with plumes of black and white smoke, made by the bursting shells.

Nothing else happened till evening. The night was less mo-notonous, for, in spite of the pitiless moonlight, one could go out. We looked on with much interest at a raid by two aero-planes, which marked down an enemy's trench and a supply convoy with luminous bombs. An instant afterwards the "75's" hit hard. Towards midnight seven shots were let off from the listening post. I said to myself, "At last, here comes the attack." I shook up my men, benumbed with cold and sleep; but dead silence again fell.

It was freezing hard enough to split stones. Over a surface of several kilometres the newly formed ice cracked and made one

A mounted scout in the Battle of Champagne, 1915

think that an advance was taking place. Little Duval, in a moment of hallucination, fired on the dead bodies, mistaking them for skirmishers.

From time to time an imperceptible breeze distinctly brought us the sound of the enemy at work. We heard the blows of mallets, used doubtless to consolidate his wire entanglements. I made our freezing men do the same.

M. Chatelin and I walked up and down or made reconnaissances simply for the sake of keeping on the move. On the plain I stumbled on the body of a dragoon between two frozen pools. His head was wrapped up in hay, but he was frozen so hard that we could not move him. I tried to lift him by his belt, but it broke in my hands. Two cats, a white one and an Angora, seemed annoyed at being deranged. Oh, the horror of it!

Décatoire had his feet frostbitten and was unable to walk. M. Chatelin and I returned to the trench, and, huddled up one against the other, we passed the remaining hours of that trying night in shivering.

At five o'clock the 5th Chasseurs relieved us.

★★★★★★

Long weeks followed, during which the cavalry, become useless on account of the time of year and the novel trench warfare, remained inactive far from the front in muddy rest-camps.

Officers and men were sent by turns into the trenches for eight or ten days at a time, being taken there in motor omnibuses.

When we returned to regimental headquarters, we led an ordinary barrack life there. The admirable unity which made us all brothers in the firing line had a tendency to relax in face of the pettiness of ordinary military duty. Peace-time jealousies showed themselves during our forced inactivity, when our tour of service did not call us far from our horses to dismounted fighting.

For this reason, and as I was desirous of living again and renewing acquaintance with those intoxicating hours to which one becomes accustomed as a necessary factor in life, preferring, in short, to perform the duties of a footsoldier with real infantry men, knowing their duties and suitably equipped, rather than to degenerate into a dismounted dragoon, I asked to be appointed 2nd Lieutenant in an infantry regiment as soon as the ministerial circular concerning cavalry non-commissioned appeared. Fifteen days later my request was granted.

I was gazetted 2nd Lieutenant on February 3rd. The 22nd were at Volckerinkove. M. de Vesian told me of my appointment, and a few hours later I was sent with the others who had been recently promoted—Fuéminville, Marin and Paris—to the headquarters of the 5th Division, and from there to Poperinghe to the headquarters of the 9th Army Corps.

In spite of my decision, taken freely of my own accord, I was very sorry to leave the 22nd. It was for me a page turned over, something finished. I passed down the ranks and shook hands with all those comrades by whose side I had marched, slept and fought for six months, and then, without looking behind me, I set off on horseback on a fine sunny day.

Having been posted to the 90th Regiment of the Line, I followed a course of instruction at Vlamertinghe, with the newly gazetted officers from Saint-Cyr. After fifteen days of a monotonous and tranquil life the class broke up on the 21st. On the morning of the 22nd I rejoined the 90th, and the same evening we left to go into action.

In February I was again in the trenches, those which I occupied affording me great amusement. We left at half-past eight in the morning, and we had eighteen kilometres to march. At Ypres we made a few minutes' halt on the edge of the pavement before the celebrated Cloth Hall. I looked eagerly around me, wishing to fix the sights which met my eyes. They were intensely picturesque and of peculiar interest. When the war is over shall we ever again see such a picture? It is not likely.

Night had come. It was a time propitious for reliefs, hence everywhere feverish activity reigned. All lights in the town were masked. Under a moon, luminous as shining chalk, the cathedral and the Cloth Hall were of a dazzling white, which made the gaping wounds which the shells have made in the stonework all the blacker and more apparent.

The scudding clouds masked the moon for a moment, and

everything faded from view, or rather, as in a kaleidoscope, the ever-changing shadows changed the forms of the ruins. Sudden beams of light rested for a moment like furtive phantoms on the stonework, to disappear a second later. On the edge of the horizon star shell were being thrown up, pitting the night with a white or green fixed star, or appearing as a diamond spray held by some invisible hand, to sparkle a moment and then vanish. The silence was cut by the regular cadence of the march of the various companies towards the neighbouring sectors.

They debouched from every cross-road. There were French, Belgians and English, the latter whistling in chorus, "It's a long, long way to Tipperary," and keeping step to it. As soon as they saw us by common accord, they started the *Marseillaise*—a charming courtesy—and strange and rapid dialogues were exchanged between the "*poilus*" and the "Tommies" in a language so untranslatable, so indescribable, that most of the men burst out laughing at hearing themselves speak. Then some guns crossed the *place* at the trot making a deafening noise.

Every unit had its destination, its appointed place and perfect order prevailed. Those back from the trenches are glad at the prospect of rest; those going there are light-hearted also, and so the active ant-heap swarms with busy people.

From time to time shell would fall in the town, crumbling still further the marvellous Cloth Hall or causing irreparable damage to the humble house of some inoffensive civilian. It was stupid and useless.

From Zonnebeck onwards the ground was swept by rifle fire, and we had to cross a horseshoe sector exposed to fire from all sides. It was impossible to find cover, and the relief was extremely difficult and dangerous. Then it was that I made acquaintance with the new and the unknown.

New trenches, new customs. We groped our way through a little pine wood. Every now and then a bullet struck the trunk of a tree with such a loud and sharp sound that the drum of one's ear was all but torn. Insensibly the company advanced along the cutting which got deeper and deeper underground. Soon one was in up to the shoulders, and the deeper the communication trench got the deeper we got into mud and water. I pretended to myself that we were figures in some "attraction" at Luna Park or the Magic City. We were in a labyrinth which turned to the right and left, doubled back on itself and got deeper and more difficult at each step, while "the bees" passed whistling over our heads.

There was a sudden stop, just as I had given up hope of ever seeing the end. The section in front of me emerged into a trench, and a ray of light fell on the wet clay at my feet. A form leaned out of a hole, and a voice said to me, "This way, sir; this is your command post." Hardly had I entered when the curtain which masked the door fell again, to shut in the light.

I found myself in a tiny square room constructed entirely of rough logs, that is to say of the trunks of pine trees. It was buried under a mountain of earth, very solidly beaten down, and it had a brick fireplace in which a good coke fire blazed (within 100 metres of the enemy). There was a bed, or rather a straw mattress, which exactly filled up the middle of this "*casba.*" The other half was taken up by a stand on which were ranged miscellaneous objects—gum boots, tin boxes, grenades, petards, flares, etc. One could not stand up, but lying down one felt like a king.

The network of trenches which unites the sections was so complicated that I lost myself in it every time. In the early morning I made a reconnaissance of the neighbouring sections. At places the parapet became so low that, even by stooping, one was not completely under cover. My presence was hailed by a salvo which passed whistling over my head.

*24th February, 1915,*—It snowed last night. The trenches are white and my "*poilus*" are cold. And so am I! A man of my section has just been wounded in the head by a bullet which ricocheted off a bayonet. But, generally speaking, the Germans leave us in peace.

*Six o'clock.*—My trench has been demolished in part by a "105." We shall have to work all night to repair it.

*26th February, 1915,*—Under cover of fog I left my shelter and had some wire entanglements made. The men were able to work without drawing fire. *Per contra* a German patrol came exploring, counting on the fog for concealment. Having arrived opposite Règues's section, they must have lost their way and pitched straight on to us. We hit three of them. All the morning, fifty metres off, we saw them wriggling and raising their legs, and we heard them crying out. It was impossible to go to bring them in, the Germans would have fired on us.

One of them signalled that he was ready to surrender. He put up his hands and cried, "*Kamarad, Kamarad*," so he can't be badly wounded. We could see him rise, unbuckle his belt and throw off his pack. My men, very pleased, were ready to receive him with open arms, but he regained his own lines at a bound. We let off a salvo, but the "*Kamarad*" had already disappeared. The two others kept on wriggling like worms.

*2nd March, 1915.*—I am occupying a new sector, not nearly so good as the first; trench fallen in, full of water, communications difficult, no comfortable command post; I sleep on the hard ground in the cold. My predecessor, when giving me my instructions, warned me that for two days past we had been badly shelled.

*3rd March,*—At 8.30 the first shell, a "105," came over and pitched some metres from my post. I was almost thrown out of the dug-out; earth and mud flew in all directions, and shell fragments fell with a sharp noise. Some moments after a second one came over, then a third and then, for three-quarters of an hour, they fell without ceasing.

All the shells fell on my left. The men were a little pale in face of this form of danger, against which there is nothing to be done. After a quarter of an hour the trench became untenable, the shelters, the parapets, the dugout, were all tumbling down. Sometimes the shock and the displacement of air threw us in bunches one against the other.

I remained at the command post until the next dug-out was knocked to pieces, burying a man under the ruins. I then caused the whole section to be evacuated, except by a watcher, and I asked hospitality from a 2nd lieutenant of machine-guns.

At last the storm calmed down and I sent everyone back to

his place. The trench was a veritable timber yard, and rifles and mess tins littered the ground. The parapet by the side of my shelter was knocked down level with the ground, leaving a gaping opening that we must repair tonight.

*Six o'clock,*—After the tension of such a morning I heard with pleasure the cry of "Stand to your arms." Each man flew to his rifle; they too, I think, were pleased. I had gone back to see my comrade the machine-gunner, but it did not take me long to cover the thirty or forty metres of trench which separated me from my men.

How good a thing it was to hear this crackle of rifle fire after the disquieting row of the "105's"! "Stand to the machine-gun." I saw with pleasure the four men at their gun, and I admired the graceful movement of the man who crouched to fire and who, unconsciously, assumed the posture of an animal ready to spring. Unfortunately, the enemy were not "for it." At our first shots the Germans got back into their trenches.

*27th March,*—We arrived yesterday in the second line, or rather in reserve. The huts are in a pine wood, surrounded with ridges. We arrived by moonlight. The bullets passed high and struck the tops of the trees. These huts are in the form of a redskin's *wigwam*, made of earth and sacking. Today we went hunting with revolvers and we killed a rabbit! We cooked it ourselves and enjoyed it for dinner.

*28th March,*—The enemy leaves us in peace. Not a shell, not the least little "77." We went hunting again and brought back a pheasant. After supper Maugenot and I intend to go and play cards with Captain Lametz, a little in front of our trenches. We must cross a glacis in front of the ridge; the bullets come over there head high. We slipped along the edge of the wood to take advantage of the lie of the land; and then all at once we said, "So much the worse," and we crossed the field at its widest part. We jumped the parapet of an old trench and we arrived at the 1st company. Captain Lametz has his post buried in a wood.

We played, seated cross-legged on the ground, by candle-light. The rest of the post were asleep, rolled up in blankets. The moonlight peered into the dug-out each time that the wind blew aside the canvas of the tent. In coming back Maugenot and I were almost stopped by bullets, chance bullets, be it understood, which fell with regularity and in disconcerting abundance, often, as they struck the ground, hitting some shell fragments which would ring like glasses knocked together.

To save time Maugenot suggested taking a short cut, and he succeeded in entangling us in an inextricable network of barbed wire. It was too late to draw back, we had to jump and crawl. We arrived, however, at the hut safe and sound, but our greatcoats were badly torn.

*29th March,*—A man had been killed some little time ago. While I write I am looking at the *cortège* which has brought him back. The body, a little bent, is carried on an improvised stretcher by four men and is wrapped up in the canvas of a tent, tinted red where it has touched his wound. The little procession advances with difficulty in the narrow communication trench, and every two or three steps a drop of blood falls and stains the ground like a star, brown-red, and the *cortège* may be traced by these as far as the grave.

Such was the daily life of almost the whole army during the winter months. Though monotonous, I have thought it well to transcribe these few passages from my daily journal, for they are human documents. In spring the benumbed army stirred itself, stretched its legs and awoke to the fact that a new era was about to begin. The change took place with the greatest mystery. News, come no one knew whence, began to circulate.

When we left Belgium on the 30th March some extravagant hypotheses took shape. Haute-Alsace, the Argonne, the Dardanelles and Turkey were spoken of. The least bellicose would have it that we were to rest near Lyons; but no one knew anything, and each day we went farther south-west, being ignorant even of the billets we would occupy that evening.

So, we passed Saint-Omer, Arneke, Pilens, Blingel, Frévent, Avesne-le-Comte, etc. . . . and we approached Arras, whose town hall and belfry we saw one morning profiled in a blue haze against a spectral sky.

On passing through Arneke on the 8th of April we marched past General Foch headed by our band. When the regiment had passed by, he sent for the officers. We were all presented to him, and he had us formed up in a circle to say a few words to us.

Listening to the general was like experiencing a species of shock. He hammered out his words and scanned his phrases in a manner which made us feel ill at ease. His speech was a flagellation, and we felt a sort of moral abasement as a result of it. His look seized upon and held us. He brought us to bay and then crushed us.

First, he spoke to us of our mission, of the utility of training the men in view of the coming fatigues.

Train their arms, train their legs, train their muscles, train their backs. You possess fine qualities, draw on them from the soles of your feet, if necessary, but get them into your heads. I have no use for people who are said to be animated by good intentions. Good intentions are not enough; I want people who are determined to get there and who do.

There are shreds of his phrases that remain graven on my memory, curt short phrases, punctuated by a sharp gesture, or by an indescribable look of the eye:

If you want to overturn that wall, don't blunt your bayonet point on it; what is necessary is to break it, shatter it, overturn it, stamp on it and walk over the ruins, *for we are going to walk over ruins*. If we have not already done so—(and here he suddenly lowered his voice and gave it an intonation almost mysterious)—*it is because we were not ready*. We lacked explosives, bombs, grenades, *minenwerfers*, which now we have. And we are going to be able to strike, *for we have a stock* such as you cannot even have an idea of. We are going to swamp the enemy, strike him everywhere at once: in his defences, in his morale, harass him, madden him, crush him; we will march over nothing but ruins.

Then he went off quite naturally, without any theatrical effect. He said just what he had to say, and he did not add a word too many. He saluted us: "I hope, gentlemen, to have the honour of seeing you again." A moment later his motorcar was carrying him off towards Cassel, leaving us deeply stirred and impressed by his spoken words and no less influenced by his personality.

# Chapter 7

# The Attack at Loos

### 9TH MAY, 1915

On April the 29th, ten days before the attack, we were taking our last great rest at Noyelette in a setting which resembled a scene from a comic opera. The apple trees were in full bloom and the blossom fell like snow. In the radiant peace of early spring we lay on the scented grass, listening to the ripples on the little stream. For many of us it was destined to be a last pleasure and a last caress which Nature was pleased to lavish on those of her children who were about to die.

★★★★★★

*6th May: In the first line,*—We relieved the 256th in the first-line trenches near Mazingarbe, on the road to Lens. That relief by a reserve regiment confirmed the rumour of an offensive. As we passed through Noeux-les-Mines and Mazingarbe even the civilians said to us, "Sure enough you are going to attack, aren't you? See to it that you push them back once and for all!"

*7th May.*—The great moment, so long expected, has come. Tomorrow the 10th Army is going to attack on the Lille-Arras front. My battalion is to advance straight forward with Hill 70 for objective on this side of Loos. I made a reconnaissance of the sector. Tonight, I am going to inspect the German barbed-wire entanglements with Stivalet. I am quite calm and very well prepared; my only fear is that I may do badly and commit some fault. That the men will go forward, I am sure. My battalion forms the first line, the 2nd and the 3rd come next, then the

125th and the 68th line regiments, while the 256th and the 281st are on the right and left and are to converge to a point.

*Two o'clock p.m.*—The French guns are beginning to shell the enemy. The batteries are landing shell just in front of our trench and so near that I am beginning to think that there must be an error in the range. The mere fact of having to wait is a torture, to know nothing and to say, "Is it to be in five minutes, this evening or tomorrow?" My heart beats hard and my throat is dry. I would give anything for the order to attack, for I know that then I should at once recover my calm.

The four sections have orders to advance to their front towards the Lens road, to take the German trenches and then make for Hill 70 by way of Loos. I distributed some asphyxiating bombs, hand grenades to my section, and little bags containing cotton previously soaked in a bisulphite and which must be dipped again into lime water at the last moment and introduced into the mouth and nostrils to neutralise the effects of asphyxiating gas.

*Four o'clock.*—The shelling is still going on, but it has lost the unheard-of violence with which it started. The remainder of the guns are to arrive tonight and consequently the attack cannot take place before tomorrow.

Everyone is at work; the Engineers are making steps and finishing saps; Artillerymen walk about in the communication trenches with range-finders with which they accomplish mysterious rites, asking me politely to move as I am in the way. Officers of all battalions are reconnoitring the sector, and the men are sewing bits of white canvas on their packs so that they may be recognised at a distance by our artillery. One would say that a costume play was in course of being mounted and that the last preparations were being made for the opening performance.

At ten minutes to nine I returned to my command post. I examined my revolver carefully, took off my tunic and put my money and my papers in my trousers pocket. I slipped my cloak on over my shirt, put my revolver in the inside pocket and I got out of the trench. I gave a last warning to my men not to fire, even if they heard firing.

Stivalet was there; we got over the parapet at nine o'clock exactly, and we had chosen a bit of known ground between two *chevaux de frise*. It was very dark; scarcely had we started than a star shell lit up the sky. We threw ourselves flat on the ground on our faces. I felt the wet grass and moist soil on my cheeks and on the palms of my hands. I listened to my breathing and I could not feel the beatings of my heart. I was perfectly calm.

For two or three minutes we groped our way across the wire of the *chevaux de frise*. When we had passed it, we came on an old network of rusted barbed wire all broken up by shell fire, and our feet and cloaks got entangled in it. We crawled on our hands and knees and each time that a star shell burst we threw ourselves flat, as before.

The critical moment had arrived. Stivalet hailed me in a low voice, "This is a rotten trip we are making," He whispered in my ear, "It is too dark, we shall see nothing."

I said to him, "All right, you stay here, I am going farther on."

I crawled on alone. I felt perturbed at being alone in the black night with all these rifle muzzles pointed at me. I was at the mercy of a flare. I went on as well as I could, without a sound, trying to blend with the ground. I went on for I don't know how long or how far. Then I looked up and I saw the German entanglements close beside me. I distinctly heard talking going on; unfortunately, I did not understand a word of it. There was no object in delaying further, my mission was over.

I had seen their defences; they were only *chevaux de frise,* united by barbed wire. As I turned, two rockets went off and crossed. I thought that I was lost and I stayed still with my head on my arms and my face to the ground, biting the grass; but nothing happened; not a shot was fired.

I started off then to crawl with a speed which astonished myself, using my feet, shoulders and elbows to help me along. I arrived at the spot where I had left Stivalet, and in no time we had jumped back into our trench. My clothes were so caked with mud that they stuck to me like a jersey. I made a report to Maugenot, whom I found asleep. On the table of the dug-out was a note from the major. The attack was to take place tomorrow. The day would be given over to a minute reconnaissance of the sector, and everything would be ready for the attack, to take place probably during the night of the 8th-9th.

*8th May, 1915.*—Unless counter-ordered the attack is to take place tomorrow at six in the morning, after four consecutive hours of shell fire. There are a thousand guns behind us, one for every fifty metres of terrain to be battered.

Nothing happened during the morning. New bombs were given out, and each man was to have at least one. From two in the afternoon the artillery corrected its shooting, which is equivalent in ordinary times to a very violent bombardment.

From my parapet I followed the phases of this correction. The redan on the Lens road blew up at two o'clock; the defences before my trench were knocked to bits. At this moment, 6.40, the artillery fired a little short. The men in the trench could not get on with their dinners; they were covered with earth and little bits of steel, and the water fatigue had some splinters sent among them—two men of the 5th were wounded.

I have got for my section 7 asphyxiating bombs, 9 Beszzi bombs, 48 hand grenades and 5 terrible chedite bombs, which I have primed myself, and of which I intend to carry two.

What a carnage is being prepared for tomorrow! I remembered the prophecy of Father Johannes, "*Only the great princes and the great captains will be buried; there will be so many dead and wounded that the bodies will be burnt on pyres whose flames will mount to the skies.*"

*9th May, 1915, 4.30 a.m.*—I am ordered to line up my men. A company of Engineers has joined us in order to excavate a communicating trench as soon as we have cleared out. Far away on the left—probably from the English lines—the guns are firing without interruption. It sounds like a hoarse roar.

5.15 and no order to attack has been received; it seems long in coming.

The guns were still thundering on the left, but ours were silent. I would give a lot to know!

*Seven o'clock.*—Orders have come; we are to attack at 10 o'clock precisely. There is to be no signal; all our watches have been synchronised. We are all to start together from our trenches at the same time. We shelled the enemy violently for an hour, but, as that was too little, we are going to shell them again from 9 to 10. The big winged bombs made a thunderous din; we could see them rise in the air like shuttlecocks and fall lightly to earth again. They looked as though they were going to rebound, but they burst at once, each like a miniature volcano in eruption.

For the second time I was astonished to find myself so calm. I could not realise that in so short a time (what are two hours?) there was going to be a wild rush, a hand-to-hand fight, hideous and disfigured corpses everywhere, and perhaps death for me. I had only the fixed idea that everything was going well. I was acutely conscious that I was responsible for the lives of fifty men.

★★★★★★

Though wounded at the beginning of the attack, and sole survivor of all the officers of the company and of a neighbouring company of the 114th regiment of the line, I was, nevertheless, still able to carry on till 8 o'clock at night.

At 9 o'clock a.m. I precipitated the ammoniacal solution and all the men soaked their pads in it. Everyone had his bomb. While I was finishing these last preparations shells and bombs seemed to crush the enemy's lines. The noise was deafening and the smoke suffocating and blinding. I should like to shut my eyes and pass in review each scene which followed, forgetting none. In a few moments I consider that I lived the sum total of a lifetime.

At a quarter to ten all were lined up, pack on back. The section of Engineers stuck to the communicating trench so as not to hinder our movements. I placed myself in the centre and took out my watch; still ten minutes to go! I called in a loud voice, "Five minutes," "Two minutes." I had a stealthy look at the men and I saw on their faces so tense an expression, something so fixed, that they seemed to be in a trance.

As I cried, "Only half a minute more!" I saw the left of the company starting off; they had some metres start of me. At all costs we must keep touch, so I shouted, "Forward," and ran straight at the German line, without seeing or hearing anything. I had a vague consciousness that the "75" guns had not yet increased their range, but we were no longer our own masters. Thousands of men, their minds fixed on the same purpose, rushed forward blindly.

As I arrived at the first German entanglement I turned round. Everyone had followed; the men were at my heels. A second later we were leaping over the parapet of the enemy's first line. I yelled, "Don't get into the communicating trench; the trench is empty, except for a few stragglers; get on and seize the second line."

The blue cloaks bounded forward together and the bayonets shone under a burning sun, for there was not a cloud in the sky.

Now, with our heads down, we entered the zone of Hell.

There is no word, sound or colour that can give an idea of it. To prevent our advance the Germans had made a barrier of fire, and we had to go through a sort of suffocating vapour. We went through sheaves of fire, from which burst forth percussion and time shells at such short intervals that the soil opened every moment under our feet. I saw, as in a dream, tiny silhouettes, drunk with battle, charging through the smoke.

The terrified Germans, caught between their own artillery fire and our bayonets, sprang up from everywhere; some cried for mercy; others turned round like madmen, whilst others again threw themselves upon us to drive us back.

Shells had made ravages in the ranks. I saw groups of five or six crushed and mown down. I caught a momentary glimpse of Petit, the corporal, at the head of a group of men, and I forgot everything else and shouted to him, "Go it: bravo, Petit!" His Herculean figure, moulded in a woollen jersey, was standing on a hillock, wielding his rifle like a windmill. Careless of shot and shell, his terrible bayonet running with blood, he seemed the very incarnation of the war. All my life I shall see him, bareheaded, covered with blood and sweat, leading the others on to carnage; and the blue sky behind.

My section and I kept pressing on, and we were now within

a few metres of the last of the German lines. At every step grey uniforms now surged. I discharged my revolver to right and left. Cries and moans rose and fell in the infernal din of that struggle.

In a second we should be occupying the enemy's last positions. What remained of my section followed me blindly. I put my foot on the parapet and cried, "Forward, lads, here we are!" then I felt as though someone had suddenly given me a brutal blow in the back with the butt-end of a rifle. I let go my revolver and the chedite bomb, which I had in my left hand, and I rolled to the bottom of a shell hole.

I was hit!

In a flash I remembered a phrase of my orderly's, overheard by chance yesterday, "If anything happens to the little lieutenant he won't be left behind," and a moment later this brave fellow, himself wounded in the arm, was at my side, and with two or three others, carried me to the trench. In front of us nothing was left, not a defence, not a wire entanglement. We had carried the German lines to their uttermost limits.

We at once set to work to dig ourselves in, whilst the men who were not digging kept a look-out. We asked ourselves from what direction the Germans would try to outflank us, for we knew nothing about the trenches that had been carried. All at once I saw two of them coming out of a little communicating trench with their bayonets at the charge. I blew out the brains of the first; the second, a veritable lad of about sixteen, had a terrified expression which I shall never forget. He yelled, and his strident cries made me shudder; but my pistol went off, and he fell on the ground on his face.

During the whole of the attack I had not for an instant seen my company commander, and I wondered where he was. My colour-sergeant told me that the major and he had been killed, that Lieutenant Desessart was badly wounded and that Lieutenant Règues and I were the only officers left in the company. Règues took command, and, seated on the parapet, superintended the preparations for defence. The guns were silent. . . . Alone the whistle of bullets was heard, and warning cries were raised: "Look out on the left; look out on the right; they are

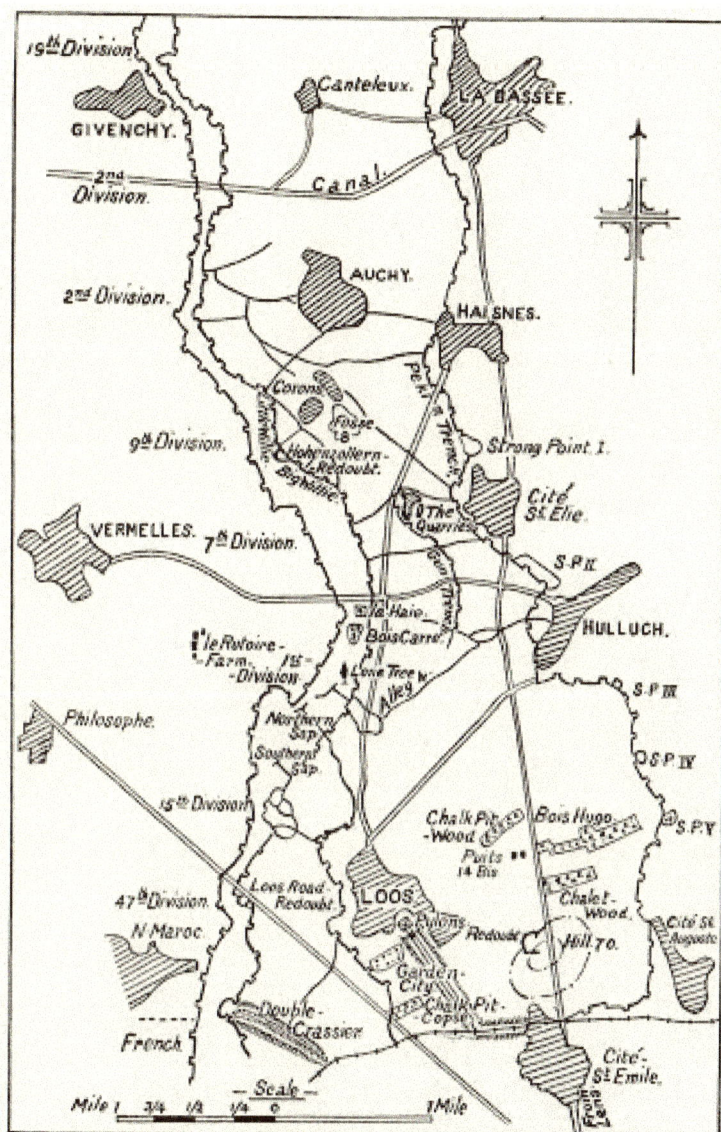

THE BATTLE OF LOOS.

coming from such and such a trench."

Then a bullet struck Règues fair on the head. He rolled over at my feet, and the sole command devolved on me. I myself was wounded; the blood was running from my back, and my movements were paralysed. My men wanted me to go back, but I stiffened myself up with the energy of despair. Someone passed me a flask of ether and I propped myself against the parapet. I was alone in command; I had all my faculties about me, and I determined to stay there whatever happened.

Up till two o'clock nothing did happen. We feverishly dug shelters to fire from, and made traverses to protect the trench which was in part open to enfilade. As far as the road everything had gone well, but, from that point on, connection was broken. The rest of the 90th were behind and parallel with me, some metres off; the Germans there had retained their positions. Though we could not see them, they were there quite near, concealed, gone to earth but ready to spring on us.

Lying almost helpless at the foot of the trench I gave my orders, which the men, one and all, carried out with remarkable presence of mind. Enervating hours slowly slipped by. The sun scorched the trench; some of the bodies took on a deep yellow colour, and their wounds were horrible.

To stop our reinforcements the Germans pitched shells behind the first lines. In the communicating trenches, where the Engineers, the 125th and the 68th, were massed, they must, I felt, be having a hot time. Even in the trench shells fell both before and behind. I had three men killed. Grossain had his head carried away.

With midday came some relaxation. Work eased off a little; the men rummaged in their haversacks; Pillard brought me some cigars, Henry Clays, and some Egyptian cigarettes. Mayet dressed my wound in a summary fashion, passing his hand through the rent in my cloak. The opening was as big as my fist. I suffered horrible pain.

The sergeant and I, nevertheless, explored the captured sector. The trenches have been knocked in by shell. In certain places it was open ground for 25 metres; in other parts corpses obstructed the way. As we went by, some Germans, lying on their backs right in the sun, opened their eyes and said, "*Ich durste.*" We had no time to stop, the guns might open fire again at any moment, and it was essential to find some means of communicating with the colonel.

When I got back to my men, I found nothing changed. Mayet, fine fellow that he is, was keeping a good look-out. The trench which barred the road was consolidated, and we placed a machine-gun in it. I took under my command a company on my left, as it had no officer left.

At half-past one a kind of agitation, a tremor, ran from man to man, as if the whole company had received an electric shock; yet there was no cry, no shot fired. Yet everyone realised that the counter-attack was about to be launched.

I was amazed at the gaiety and good humour which prevailed. I wanted to say a few words regarding their conduct, but there was little need to sustain their morale. They shut me up by shouting, "Long live the lieutenant." I was too overcome with emotion to reply.

All of a sudden there came a burst of musketry. It was sharp and brutal, and there was no hesitation about it. One felt that it was not the sort of musketry fire that one might expect from dispirited men, firing without taking the trouble to aim; on the contrary, each shot had its target. I looked through my field-glasses in its direction; it was on my left, about three hundred metres off.

The Germans, who were masters of a communication trench in front of us, debouched from it and tried to rush us in column of fours. They did not gain an inch of ground. Each section of fours was shot down.

One cannot but render homage to such soldiers. A whole company was wiped out, not a man rose again after he fell, not a man retreated. The second counter-attack took shape on the right under the same conditions. The Germans were massed in a communication trench parallel to the road. A little later, again on the left, the enemy profited by a small wood to concentrate his men and to attempt a sortie, and this again was stopped short.

They seemed to have resigned themselves to doing what we were doing. By the aid of a periscope we could see them as far as their waist-belts. They were smoking and waiting.

To put one's head up was to court death. Maugenot was lying just beyond the parapet on the grass with his face to the ground. Already he was the colour of wax. I determined to have him picked up at night.

The colonel, at three o'clock, sent me the 7th company, under Captain Dupont, as a reinforcement. I told him that I wanted to stay where I was. That it was I and my men who had taken this ground, and therefore that it was ours by right; so, the captain settled down on the right, and at least I was no longer alone.

I could gain no clue as to the real state of affairs from the complete silence of the German artillery. There was a noise of waggons coming and going on the higher ground, and this seemed to me to mean a fresh supply of munitions. It was unfortunately impossible to communicate with our own artillery.

Seated at the bottom of the trench, I began to feel my senses deserting me. When I was asked for orders, I racked my brains in vain. I could not find the right thing to say. I tried to joke with the men, but profound melancholy possessed me, for I began to realise that I was no longer good for anything.

At 7 o'clock at night came the order for the attack which was preparing.

The 3rd battalion will carry out the attack on the village of Loos, taking the steeple as directing point, and joining up on the left with the 114th. The first line units—the 3rd, 7th, 4th and 8th companies—will be pushed forward by the attacking battalion. Preparations for this movement must be made as soon as possible, but no move forward is to be made till further orders.—Signed Alquier.

Night fell rapidly. I was anxious to speak to the colonel before the new attack if I could get to him, and so I handed over command to Mayet. My wound hurt me horribly. It felt as if my left shoulder were being torn from my body, as though indeed I were being quartered. I had doubts as to whether I could get to where I should find him, but I knew what could be done if the will to do were strong. Alas! I was not to see the company again, nor was I to succeed in finding the colonel.

On the way I walked like a drunken man, staggering from one wall of the trench to the other. Sometimes I had to climb over pyramids of bodies, sometimes I had to go right outside the trench, amidst the whistling of bullets and the noise of shells, which burst on all sides. I reflected sadly on how stupid it would be to be killed there, all alone, after having so miraculously escaped during the fight. I met some men of the Engineers, some prisoners and some messengers. Everyone was in a hurry, and I automatically repeated the same phrase to each, "Look out, I am a wounded officer, don't hustle me." I asked myself if it was possible to suffer more than I did. A sort of continuous groaning sound escaped me, my sight became blurred and I walked as if in delirium.

I went round the same sector several times, asking everyone where the colonel was.

And they would ask me, "What colonel?"

I had forgotten, and then everything became vague. I met two men with fixed bayonets in charge of three prisoners. They gave me some red wine and took me along with them. We passed a factory whose broken machinery I saw profiled against the night sky. Then some stretcher-bearers picked me up and carried me to the neighbouring aid post. From there I was sent by ambulance to the divisional dressing station at Mazingarbe, where I passed the night.

The building was plunged into complete darkness for fear of being marked down. Our big guns—the 120 long—were firing quite near, and at every round the walls trembled and the window-panes rattled. One could well picture oneself still in the thick of the fight. The noise of musketry seemed to come from the garden, and I still remember clearly the sinister sights that I saw there. Dimly made out in the shadow, the wounded were lying on straw in rows on the ground. One only saw their silhouettes. There were infantrymen, artillerymen and Algerian Light: Infantry on whom the white dressings stood out sharply.

DRAGOONS AND PRISONERS OF WAR

Amidst the roar of the guns one would hear a long-drawn moan and some groans, cut short at times by incoherent phrases. All of them raved. Officers and men lived through the morning's battle once again, and brief commands were uttered, infinitely painful to listen to, "March in open order, by the right; stand by the machine-gun," and so on. As I stretched myself on some straw in the least encumbered corner, I shivered with fever. The next morning, we were all sent on to Noeux-les-Mines, and from there we left by train for we knew not where.

LEONAUR

# ALSO FROM LEONAUR
## AVAILABLE IN SOFTCOVER OR HARDCOVER WITH DUST JACKET

**THE FALL OF THE MOGHUL EMPIRE OF HINDUSTAN** *by H. G. Keene*—By the beginning of the nineteenth century, as British and Indian armies under Lake and Wellesley dominated the scene, a little over half a century of conflict brought the Moghul Empire to its knees.

**LADY SALE'S AFGHANISTAN** *by Florentia Sale*—An Indomitable Victorian Lady's Account of the Retreat from Kabul During the First Afghan War.

**THE CAMPAIGN OF MAGENTA AND SOLFERINO 1859** *by Harold Carmichael Wylly*—The Decisive Conflict for the Unification of Italy.

**FRENCH'S CAVALRY CAMPAIGN** *by J. G. Maydon*—A Special Correspondent's View of British Army Mounted Troops During the Boer War.

**CAVALRY AT WATERLOO** *by Sir Evelyn Wood*—British Mounted Troops During the Campaign of 1815.

**THE SUBALTERN** *by George Robert Gleig*—The Experiences of an Officer of the 85th Light Infantry During the Peninsular War.

**NAPOLEON AT BAY, 1814** *by F. Loraine Petre*—The Campaigns to the Fall of the First Empire.

**NAPOLEON AND THE CAMPAIGN OF 1806** *by Colonel Vachée*—The Napoleonic Method of Organisation and Command to the Battles of Jena & Auerstädt.

**THE COMPLETE ADVENTURES IN THE CONNAUGHT RANGERS** *by William Grattan*—The 88th Regiment during the Napoleonic Wars by a Serving Officer.

**BUGLER AND OFFICER OF THE RIFLES** *by William Green & Harry Smith*—With the 95th (Rifles) during the Peninsular & Waterloo Campaigns of the Napoleonic Wars.

**NAPOLEONIC WAR STORIES** *by Sir Arthur Quiller-Couch*—Tales of soldiers, spies, battles & sieges from the Peninsular & Waterloo campaingns.

**CAPTAIN OF THE 95TH (RIFLES)** *by Jonathan Leach*—An officer of Wellington's sharpshooters during the Peninsular, South of France and Waterloo campaigns of the Napoleonic wars.

**RIFLEMAN COSTELLO** *by Edward Costello*—The adventures of a soldier of the 95th (Rifles) in the Peninsular & Waterloo Campaigns of the Napoleonic wars.

www.ingramcontent.com/pod-product-compliance
Lightning Source LLC
Chambersburg PA
CBHW031858090426

42741CB00005B/549